"Your Hearts Will Rejoice"

Easter Meditations from the *Vita Christi*
by Ludolph of Saxony, Carthusian

MONASTIC WISDOM SERIES NUMBER FORTY-NINE

"Your Hearts Will Rejoice"

Easter Meditations from the *Vita Christi* by Ludolph of Saxony, Carthusian

Translated by

Milton T. Walsh

α

Cistercian Publications
www.cistercianpublications.org

LITURGICAL PRESS
Collegeville, Minnesota
www.litpress.org

A Cistercian Publications title published by Liturgical Press
Cistercian Publications

Editorial Offices
161 Grosvenor Street
Athens, Ohio 54701
www.cistercianpublications.org

Biblical citations are based on the Challoner revision of the Douay-Rheims translation of the Vulgate Bible.

1   2   3   4   5   6   7   8   9

Library of Congress Cataloging-in-Publication Data

Ludolf, von Sachsen, approximately 1300–1377 or 1378.
    [Vita Christi. Selections. English]
    Your hearts will rejoice : Easter meditations from the Vita Christi of Ludolph of Saxony, Carthusian / Ludolph the Carthusian ; translated by Milton T. Walsh.
        pages   cm. — (Monastic wisdom series ; number forty-nine)
    ISBN 978-0-87907-349-7 — ISBN 978-0-87907-331-2 (ebook)
    1. Jesus Christ—Biography—Early works to 1800.   2. Jesus Christ—Biblical teaching—Early works to 1800.   3. Easter—Meditations—Early works to 1800.   I. Walsh, Milton T., translator.   II. Title.

BT301.3.L8313   2016
232.9'7—dc23   2015034156

*So you have sorrow now, but I will see you again
and your hearts will rejoice,
and no one will take your joy from you.*

John 16:22

With gratitude to Saint Bruno's companions,
the Carthusian monks in Calabria

*waiting for the return of the master,
ready to open the door for him as soon as he knocks.*

Saint Bruno, *Letter to Raoul*, 4

Contents

Abbreviations for Works Cited

Unless further identification is needed, *Sermo* or *Hom* refers to a sermon or homily by an author, followed by its number. Numbers in brackets refer to modern critical editions that differ from the PL. When the citation is from a biblical commentary, *Com* is followed by the biblical reference, e.g., Com Matt 28:4. Bracketed references in this list refer to modern critical editions of the cited texts.

Auvergne	*Guilielmi Alverni, Opera omnia* (Paris, 1674)
Brev in Ps	Ps-Jerome, *Breviarium in Psalmos*
CA	Thomas Aquinas, *Catena aurea*
Caillau	*S. Augustini, Sermones inediti*
Caillau Aug.	Caillau, *Augustini operum* (Paris, 1836)
CCCM	Corpus Christianorum, Continuatio Mediævalis
CCL	Corpus Christianorum Latinorum
Conf	Augustine, *Confessiones* [CCL, vol. 27]
Creat	Isidore, *De ordine creaturarum* [Monografías de la Universidad de Santiago de Compostela #10]
CSEL	Corpus Scriptorum Ecclesiasticorum Latinorum
CSLP	Corpus Scriptorum Latinorum Paravianum
Cumm	Cummianus, *Commentarius in Evangelium secundam Marcam*
De civ Dei	Augustine, *De civitate Dei* [CCL vols. 47–48]
De cons ev	Augustine, *De consensu evangelistarum* [CSEL vol. 43]

De conv	Bernard, *De conversione ad clericos* [SBOp vol. 4]
De div	Bernard, *Sermones de diversis* [SBOp vol. 6]
De doc	Augustine, *De doctrina Christiana* [CCL vol. 32]
De exc	Eadmer, *De excellentia Virginis Mariae*
De fide	Augustine, *De fide et symbolo*
De inst	Aelred of Rievaulx, *De institutione inclusarum* [CCCM 1]
De laud	Arnold of Bonneval, *De laudibus Beatae Virginis Mariae*
De res carnis	Tertullian, *De resurrectione carnis*
De sym	Augustine, *Sermo de symbolo* [CCL vol. 46]
De Trin	Augustine, *De Trinitate* [CCL vols. 50–51]
De vir	Ambrose, *De virginibus* [CSLP new series vol. 18]
De vir ill	Jerome, *De viris illustribus*
Drogo	Drogo of Ostia, *Sermo de sacramento dominicae passionis*
En ev Matt, Mark . . .	Theophylact, *Enarrationes in Evangelium Matthaei, Marci*, etc.
En Ps	Augustine, *Enarrationes in Psalmos* [CCL vols. 38–40]
Ep	Epistle
Erasmus	Erasmus, *Origenis adamantii operum pars secunda* (Basel, 1545)
Ety	Isidore, *Etymologiae*
Eutropium	Chrysostom, *Oratio ad Eutropium*
Exp Acta	Theophylact, *Explicationes in Acta Apostolorum*
Exp ev Luke	Ambrose, *Expositio evangelii secundam Lucam*
Hex	Ambrose, *Hexaemeron* [CCL vol. 14]
Hist ev	Peter Comestor, *Historia evangelica*
Hom Acta	Chrysostom, *Homiliae in Acta Apostolorum*
Hom ev	Bede, *Homiliarium evangelii* [CCL vol. 122]
Hom John	Chrysostom, *Homiliae in Ioannem*

Hom Matt	Chrysostom, *Homiliae in Mattheum*
In Cant Cant I	Alan de Lille, *Compendiosa in Cantica Canticorum*
Int nom	Jerome, *Liber interpretationum hebraicorum nominum* [CCSL 72]
Lib de pas	Ps-Bernard, *Liber de passione Christi*
Liverani	F. Liverani, *Spicilegium Liberianum* (Florence, 1863)
Mar	Eusebius, *Quaestiones ad Marinum*
Med	Anselm and others, *Meditationes* [Schmitt, *S. Anselmi opera*]
Med red	Anselm, *Meditatio redemptionis humanae* [Schmitt, *S. Anselmi opera*]
Mor	Gregory the Great, *Moralium libri sive expositione in librum Iob* [CCL vols. 43–43b]
Opus imperf	Ps-Chrysostom, *Opus imperfectum in Matthaeum*
Orat	Gregory Nazianzen, *Orationes*
Oratio	Aelred of Rievaulx, *Oratio pastoralis* (CCCM 1)
PG	Migne, Patrologia Graeca (Paris, 1856)
PL	Migne, Patrologia Latina (Paris, 1844)
40 hom	Gregory the Great, *XL homiliarium in Evangelia* [CCL vol. 141]
Quatuor	Eadmer, *De quatuor virtutibus Beatae Virginis Mariae*
Reg past	Gregory the Great, *Regula Pastoralis*
Roland	Chrysostomi opera (Paris: Guillielmum Roland, 1546)
SBOp	Sancti Bernardi Opera (Rome, 1957–1963)
SC	Bernard, *Sermones super Cantica Canticorum* [SBOp vols. 1–2]
Sedulius	Sedulius, *Carmen paschale*
Selecta	Origen, *Selecta in Psalmos*
Sent	Albert the Great, *Commentarii in sententiarum*
Super unum	Peter Cantor, *Super unum ex quatuor*

Tr John ep	Augustine, *In Ioannis Epistulam tractatus*
Tr John ev	Augustine, *In Evangelium Ioannis tractatus* [CCL vol. 36]
VC	Ludolph, *Vita Christi*

Introduction

The church devotes forty days to the Lenten fast and fifty days to the Easter feast. But while there are shelves of books about our Lord's passion, there are relatively few devoted to his resurrection. What can we use for our prayer during the Easter season? Here, for the first time in English, are meditations for Easter from the *Vita Christi*, a spiritual classic of the fourteenth century. This work, written by the Carthusian Ludolph of Saxony, was an early and extremely comprehensive book of meditations on the events recorded in the gospels. The *Vita Christi* was popular for centuries, for it brought together a wealth of commentary on the life of Jesus by the fathers and saints.[1]

A Castilian translation read by Ignatius Loyola during his convalescence was instrumental in his conversion, and Teresa of Avila directed that every convent of her reform include "the Carthusian" in its library. The *Vita Christi* was read by Mary Magdalen de' Pazzi and Robert Bellarmine and was recommended to Jane Frances de Chantal by Francis de Sales.[2] Nor was its influence limited to Roman Catholic

[1] There is no critical edition of the *Vita Christi*. The text used for this translation is Ludolphus de Saxonia, *Vita Jesu Christi*, ed. L. M. Rigollot (Paris: Victor Palmé, 1870).

[2] Ignatius of Loyola, "Reminiscences" 5, in *Saint Ignatius of Loyola: Personal Writings*, trans. Joseph A Munitiz and Philip Endean (London: Penguin Books, 1996), 14; Teresa of Avila, "The Constitutions" 8, in *The Collected Works of St. Teresa of Avila*, trans. Kieran Kavanaugh and Otilio Rodriguez (Washington, DC: ICS Publications, 1985), 3:321. For information about the influence of the *Vita Christi* on many saints and authors over the centuries,

circles; Ludolph's book was a favorite among the
followers of the *Devotio Moderna*, and it is likely that
Luther and other reformers were nourished by it. The
reflections offered by Ludolph can assist us, too, as
we seek to be fed by God's word.

Ludolph follows a pattern in each of his meditations, a pattern inspired by the spiritual reading of
Scripture through a process of *lectio divina*. He begins with the biblical text itself, providing historical,
geographical, or legal background where necessary,
and invites the reader to enter imaginatively into the
event. This first step corresponds to the literal sense,
the stage of *lectio*. It is followed by an exploration
of the text along moral and spiritual lines, a *medita-
tio* providing spiritual interpretations and personal
applications. Each chapter ends in *oratio*, a prayer
that succinctly summarizes the main points of the
meditation. Ludolph does not deal explicitly with
the fourth stage, *contemplatio*. It is God's gift, not the
result of our effort. The author's intent is to ready the
soul for this profound encounter with God.

How can Ludolph help us when we open the gospels to meditate on the life of Christ, beginning with
the literal meaning of the text? It is facile to dismiss
past generations as naïve in accepting all biblical stories as literally true or, on the other hand, of being so
preoccupied with allegorical interpretations as to be
unconcerned about what really happened. It is true
that a fourteenth-century author did not possess the
historical tools at our disposal; still, Ludolph relied
extensively on the tools that were available to him.
For example, throughout the *Vita Christi*, he makes
use of guidebooks to the Holy Land. He gives the

---

see Mary Immaculate Bodenstedt, *The* Vita Christi *of Ludolph the
Carthusian*, in *Ludolphus the Carthusian:* Vita Christi, *Introductory
Volume* (Salzburg: Analecta Cartusiana, 2007), v–160, here 53–92.

reason in his Prologue: "This is why sometimes I describe the locations where events took place: when we read in the gospel that this or that action happened in a certain place, it is very helpful to know something about where it occurred."[3]

Along with using historical resources to examine the literal meaning of a passage, Ludolph sometimes does something more audacious: he interpolates phrases into the biblical texts he quotes. For example, *"And he said to them: 'Why are you troubled, and why do thoughts arise from* the false and fantastic depths of *your* weak and wavering *hearts*, rather than descending from the true and good heights of heaven?'"[4] Why does he make these insertions? People in his day knew a good part of the gospels by heart; by adding phrases, he makes the passages conversational and fresh. He also supplies concrete details that flesh out the literal meaning of the text to stimulate the readers' imaginations. He appeals to their senses: he urges them to see, to picture, to imagine, to put themselves into the scene being considered. He does all of this to enrich their reading of Christ's life, to make its events three-dimensional.

But this presentation of what happened is the prelude to a more important question: What does it mean to me now? This is where Ludolph makes the transition from reading to meditation, to a consideration of

*Luke 24:38; below, 87, chap. 9

[3] Ludolph's Prologue is cited here from Milton Walsh, "'To Always Be Thinking Somehow About Jesus': The Prologue of Ludolph's *Vita Christi*," *Studies in the Spirituality of Jesuits* 43, no. 1 (2011): 1–39, here 34. The Prologue will be available in my forthcoming translation of the entire *Vita Christi* from Cistercian Publications.

[4] Biblical citations are based on the Challoner revision of the Douay-Rheims translation of the Vulgate; Ludolph almost always cites the Vulgate, which varies at times from the original Hebrew or Greek and from modern English translations made from these.

the spiritual meaning of Scripture, urging his readers, "Read what once happened as if it were happening here and now."* To help them do this, he translates the gospel past into the present, employing liturgical ceremonies, religious customs, nature's seasons and elements, and family and social life to help readers see the life of Jesus unfolding now in their lives and in the world around them. Christ's life is not a movie; it is a script, a script that we perform. For example, Ludolph likens the priest or communicant approaching the altar to Mary Magdalen in the garden on Easter morning: "If she, who was privileged to be the first to see the risen Christ after his mother, and who was so loved by the one who had delivered her from all of her sins, was prevented from touching his feet, how much more should those who are polluted by sin refrain from touching him by celebrating Mass or receiving Holy Communion?"*

*VC Prol 34

*57, chap. 5

Although Ludolph occasionally presents allegorical interpretations, his major emphasis is on the moral lessons found in the gospel. Meditation entails going beneath the surface of the events in Christ's life to the underlying attitudes and virtues that they offer for our instruction. In effect, reading the gospels should be an exercise in ongoing conversion. He writes for ordinary believers in every state of life, and his purpose is to encourage them to ponder and make their own the virtues underlying Christ's actions. These are ordinary (albeit challenging) traits: patience, gentleness, fidelity, obedience, courage, and, above all, humility.

Meditation on the life of Christ not only makes past events present; it also reminds us that Christ himself is present and that he gives us the grace to follow his example. Awareness of his presence moves us from meditation to prayer. Ludolph suggests this transition in different ways. He concludes each chapter with a brief prayer, ordinarily addressed to Christ, which summarizes the major themes of that chapter, and he occasionally introduces a prayer into his text. All these prayers, both those within the text and those at the end of each meditation, here appear in italics.

Another of Ludolph's techniques is to urge the reader to pause and identify emotionally with Jesus or other figures in the story. This is not just an impetus to respond on an emotional level to the gospel scene; it is an invitation to converse familiarly with Christ, who is present. Because this conversation is an intimate matter, Ludolph does not spell out the dialogue; he simply invites us to have it. In the stages of reading and meditating, we exercise an active role, whereas in prayer we allow Christ to speak and act. To the extent that we open ourselves to grace, frequent, prayerful meditation on the life of Christ can enable us to see Christ in everything and everyone in this world.

And beyond this world? Ludolph says that praying the life of Christ "marks the beginning of that profound contemplation we long for in the angelic, eternal life of our true homeland." * Jesus' life did not end in death, nor will ours: "If you have followed him for a little while on earth with a godly, humble, and loving heart, he in turn will raise you up to sit with him at the right hand of God the Father in heaven, just as he promised the faithful sinner who clings to him: *'If any man minister to me, let him follow me, and where I am, there also shall my minister be.'"* *

*VC Prol 25

*John 12:26; VC Prol 25–26

Although Ludolph produced a meticulously detailed *Life of Christ*, we know little of his own life. It is believed that he was a Dominican friar for many years. He entered the Carthusian monastery near Strasbourg in 1340, serving in various capacities in that order. He died at the Charterhouse at Strasbourg on April 13, 1378. He has been credited with several works (even, incorrectly, the *Imitation of Christ*), but the two major writings surely from his pen are an *Exposition on the Psalms* and his most influential book, the *Vita Christi*. This magisterial work presents the entire sweep of the life of Christ, from the eternal generation of the Son through his incarnation, ministry, death, and resurrection, concluding with the Last Judgment. Ludolph can best be understood as a masterful editor rather than an original author: he assembled an encyclopedic resource, drawing extensively on the fathers, later spiritual writers, and contemporary sources. He cites nearly eighty Christian and secular writers and incorporates passages from many other authors.

Ludolph shows great care in citing his sources. Writing long before the use of quotation marks was adopted, he always introduces a citation by giving the author's name and nearly always repeats it at the end of the quotation (e.g., *haec Anselmus*). It is also noteworthy that his citations are extremely faithful to the original works—testimony to his care and that of generations of copyists over many centuries.

The present volume serves as an introduction to the entire *Life of Christ* by Ludolph, which is being prepared for publication by Cistercian Publications. This will mark not only the first time this important text will be available in English, but also the first version of the *Vita Christi* in any language that identifies virtually all the sources used by Ludolph in producing a work that the noted Benedictine medieval scholar André Wilmart called "one of the most beautiful and erudite works to have come down to us from the Middle Ages."[5]

---

[5] André Wilmart, "Le Grand Poème Bonaventurien sur les Sept Paroles du Christ en Croix," *Revue bénédictine* 47 (Denée [Bel]: Abbaye de Maredsous, 1935): 235–78, here 268.

1

Prologue
Holy Saturday

The Sabbath morning found our Lady and her companions at home with John, behind locked doors. As they discussed all the tragic events of the day before, grief and sadness overwhelmed them; when they fell silent, they simply looked at one another and wept, as mourners do. One by one the disciples arrived, each of them also in tears. When there was a pause in the weeping, each apostle admitted sorrowfully that he had proven untrue and had abandoned the Lord. They recollected all that the Lord had done for them, first one, then another in turn. Contemplate them attentively and enter into their sorrow, for they are suffering greatly. They do not know what to do or how to comfort each other except by recollecting what the Lord had said and done.

Our Lady, however, remained at peace and tranquil in her heart: her hope in her Son's resurrection was unshakeable. On that Sabbath the faith of the church remained in her alone, and we honor her on Saturdays for this reason. Augustine says, "The Virgin grieved over the unjust death of her Son, but at the same time she firmly believed and trusted that once he had conquered death, Jesus would rise again on the third day as he had promised."*[1] During those

*Ps-Bernard, Lib de pas; PL 182:1139B

[1] The custom of celebrating Mass on Saturday in honor of our Lady goes back to the ninth century. The idea that Mary alone kept faith after her son's death is found in Alan de Lille (d. 1185), *In Cant Cant 1* (PL 210:58B), and other medieval writers.

three days she alone safeguarded the church's faith. While all the others wavered and faltered she, who had once received the gift of faith from God and had conceived by faith, never lost faith. She awaited the resurrection with certain hope. Even so, the recollection of her son's cruel and unjust death prevented Mary from rejoicing.

On the Sabbath day they rested, according to the commandment of the law, and refrained from all work, since it was prohibited to engage in any labor on that day.* For this reason, *Sabbath* is understood to mean *rest* or *pause*. Great is the dignity of the Sabbath, for on this day the whole Trinity took its repose: the Father rested from the work of creation, which he had carried out in great power; the Son rested from the work of re-creation, which he had undertaken with infinite wisdom; and the Holy Spirit rested this day with great and infinite goodness in the Virgin, for while the apostles and the women fell away from the grace of the Spirit, she remained steadfast.

And when the Sabbath was past, and the sun had set and the first stars twinkled in the evening sky, *Mary Magdalen and Mary the mother of James and Salome bought sweet spices* to make ointments, *that coming, they might anoint Jesus.** The women buy spices and make ointments to counteract the putrefaction of Christ's body, as if they have forgotten the words of the prophet: *Nor will you allow your holy one to see corruption.** Theophylact comments, "They do not yet possess the faith they should: following the Jewish custom, they prepare fragrant ointments for Jesus as if he were only human."* These holy and dedicated women followed Jesus during his life, and now in death they want to lavish care on him again. They purchase spices and prepare a balm with which to anoint the most sacred body of Jesus in the morning, since nightfall prevented them from going to

*Luke 23:56

*Mark 16:1

*Ps 15:10

*En Ev Luke 23:50-56; PG 123:1110B

the tomb. Watch them now: see how earnestly and devoutly they work, sending up sighs and tears to the Lord as they do so. They are busy throughout the night, scarcely taking any rest. Our Lady and the apostles look on, and perhaps lend a hand as best they can. If they let you, you also should help them.

Our Lord's Three Days in the Tomb

Now consider what our Lord was doing during these three days of his death. His dead body was in the tomb, his soul among the holy ancestors in limbo, and his Godhead was united to both soul and body. Leo the Great teaches, "The form of God and the form of a slave come together in a unity that can never be broken or ended. Whether it be in omnipotence or in humiliation, Christ's two natures are so united that his humanity and divinity can never be separated."* Now was fulfilled what Christ himself had predicted: *For as Jonas was in the whale's belly three days and three nights, so shall the Son of man be in the heart of the earth three days and three nights.** Augustine explains that the three days should be understood as a figure of speech in which a part is taken for the whole. Jesus lay in the tomb for the last part of Friday, all of Saturday, and the first part of Sunday; these are three natural days, if the night before is taken to be part of the day.*

Notice that the natural order of the day is here changed. Formerly, day preceded night, because day was created first, and then night, but now the creator of time has made night precede day, because the night on which he rose was joined to the day on which his resurrection was manifest. Augustine says, "Formerly days were computed from morning to evening because humankind fell from the light of grace into the darkness of sin; now we compute the day from evening to morning because, thanks to the

*Sermo 30; PL 54:234A

*Matt 12:40

*De cons ev 3.24.66; PL 34:1199

restoration effected by Christ's passion and resurrection, we move from the darkness of sin to the light
of grace."* Preaching at the Easter Vigil, Bede said,

*De Trin 4.6;
PL 42:894

> Our Lord, the author and regulator of time, rose
> from the dead in the last part of this night, trans-
> forming the whole of it into a brilliant festival by
> the light of his resurrection. From the creation of
> the world until this night, the course of time was
> divided so that day preceded night, in accord with
> its primeval making. On this night, because of the
> Lord's resurrection, the order has been reversed:
> he rose from the dead during the night, and the
> following day he showed the effects of the resur-
> rection to his disciples. Having shared a feast with
> them, he demonstrated the truth of his power, to
> their wonder and joy. Most fittingly is night now
> joined to the day that follows it, and the sequence
> of time now sees night preceding the day.*

*Hom ev
2.1 [2.7]; PL
94:135B

And Peter Cantor writes,

> In the original order of things the day was com-
> puted with the night following it, because in the
> first creation day preceded night: first, *light was
> made*, and then the darkness followed; it was *one*
> natural *day*, night following day.* Through the
> mystery of the Lord's passion the natural order
> is reversed, so that the night precedes the day.
> This is spoken of mystically in these words: *For
> you were heretofore darkness, but now light in the
> Lord*, and *the night is passed and the day is at hand.**
> The Lord chose to give a harbinger of this change
> of sequence in the law, which is why the day is
> figured from sunset to sunset when determining
> the Sabbath.*

*Gen 1:4-5

*Eph 5:8;
Rom 13:12

*Super
unum 4

Christ Descends *ad inferos*

At the hour when our Savior bowed his head and
breathed his last, his body hung on the cross, while

his soul, united to his divinity, descended to plun-
der the realm of death. As he descended, the angelic
choir went before him and broke open the gates of the
underworld. The holy people held captive in death's
thrall cried out,

> You have come, long-desired one,
> Whom we have awaited here, chained in the darkness,
> So that you could lead us out of prison.
> Our sighs have called out to you,
> Our loud laments have sought you out.
> You are the hope of the hopeless,
> The consolation of the afflicted.[2]

But what words can express the tremendous joy
when Christ, the Sun of Justice, appeared to them
and the light, so long awaited, dawned on those who
dwelled in the shadow of death? Now the Lord stood
in their midst and they were suffused with glory, for
the vision of God is perfect glory. And in that same
place stood the thief to whom Jesus had said, *"This
day you shall be with me in Paradise."* The name *Paradise* here means the enjoyment of God in the beatific
vision: now that the passion was ended, the thief
and those dwelling in limbo could see God himself.

*Luke 23:43

Christ's entrance into the underworld and the
joy of the saints there was prefigured by the three
young men cast into the furnace in Babylon, when
the angel changed the searing flames into a soothing mist. They were youths, and only the pure and
innocent abide in limbo. (Those who had died without having completed satisfaction for their sins were
first purified in purgatory before entering limbo.)
The souls in limbo are also symbolized by Daniel in

*Dan 3:25

---

[2] The *Canticum triumphale* was a medieval hymn that was often
incorporated into Holy Saturday rituals and Easter mystery plays.
It is based on Sermo 160 of Ps-Augustine (PL 39:2061).

*Dan
14:35-38
the lions' den, him whom God fed miraculously by
the prophet Habakkuk.* God kept Daniel from being
mauled by the lions and sent him food by means of
an angel; similarly, God protected the souls in limbo
from attacks by demons and at last gave them heavenly refreshment by coming to them himself.[3]

Once the author of death was vanquished, Christ
totally destroyed the devil's hold over his elect: it was
only just that, having been tricked into attacking the
Head of the Body, over which he had no rights, the
devil should forfeit power over the members of the
Body. Christ gave to us mortal creatures the reward
for all he had endured for our sake: by his passion,
the end of suffering; by his death, immortality; by
his sojourn on earth, an eternal homeland. Pope Leo
says, "The devil, that wicked thief and insatiable
tax collector, persisted in attacking the one who had
nothing of his and demanded punishment for iniq-
uity from one who had no fault. Because his claim
was unjust, the whole debt was canceled. The strong
one was bound by his own chains, and all his wicked
devices redounded on his own head. When the prince
of this world is fettered, his instruments of captivity
*Sermo 22.4;
PL 54:197B
can be seized."* Anselm writes,

> Even though the God-Man did not owe the debt
> of death, because he was sinless, he gave up his
> life for the Father's honor when this was allowed
> for the sake of justice. In his case, human nature
> gave itself to God the Father freely because he

---

[3] Albert the Great (ca.1206–1280) was the first to use the term
limbo, meaning *hem* or *border*, for the abodes of the righteous before Christ's death and of unbaptized children (Sent 4.1.20.1).
The *Limbus Patrum* grew out of patristic reflection on the events
described in this chapter; the *Limbus Puerorum* was a later Western
development, to counteract a position put forward by Augustine
in his debate with Pelagianism that unbaptized infants must be
damned. The *Limbus Puerorum* (unlike purgatory) is not a dogmatic
teaching of the church, but a theological opinion.

owed no debt of his own, and in this way others who were themselves unable to pay the debt were redeemed. Thus this man, when he freely gave himself to God, redeemed all others by assuming their debt himself. We are not freed only once by this payment; rather, we are welcomed every time we return with fitting penance.*

*Med red
3.87

According to Gregory the Great, what the Lord promised before his passion he fulfilled in his resurrection: *And I, if I be lifted up from the earth, will draw all things to myself.** Part of *all things* drawn to the Lord are the elect in limbo, whom he recognizes as his own by their faith and good works.*

*John 12:32

*40 hom 22.6;
PL 76:1177C

> *Generous Lord, you drew all things to yourself when you were lifted up from the earth with your arms outstretched on the cross. Do not, I plead, abandon me in the mud of my selfish desires; draw me to yourself to be crucified with you. Grant that I may be so dead to the world and alive to you that it may truly no longer be I who live, but you, Christ, who live in me.*

Ponder with what kindness, charity, and humility Christ descended into the realm of the dead. He could have sent an angel from heaven to release his servants and bring them to him had he wished, but his love and humility would not allow this. He went in person, and he greeted the inhabitants not just as servants but as friends and stayed with them until the dawn of Easter morning.

The Rejoicing of the Liberated Saints

Our holy ancestors rejoiced exceedingly at the Lord's coming; all misery was banished, and their hearts were full of joy. When they first saw him, they knelt in adoration. Rising to their feet, they stood before him singing songs and canticles with reverent but effusive exultation. And these praises resounded

throughout limbo all night long, with multitudes of
angelic choirs joining in the song. Mingle your voice
with theirs, adding to their melodious jubilation with
a full voice. O what a blissful and pleasant celebration
this is, even when we contemplate it from afar!

Now the true Samson had destroyed his enemies
by dying, and with his own blood the Lamb without
blemish had delivered the prisoners from the dry cistern. Now the angel had led Lot and his family out of
Sodom, leaving the wicked to be consumed in fire and
brimstone. Now the angel had devastated Egypt and
freed the Israelites. The strong man had fortified his
palace, but Christ overcame him and, vanquishing him
with his cross, bound him in chains.* This victory was
prefigured by Banaiah, who, encountering a lion in a
dry cistern, struck it down with his club; in the same
way, Christ entered the devil's lair and struck him
down with his cross.* The strong Samson, who killed
a lion with his bare hands, was a type of the strong
Christ, who overcame the satanic beast and freed his
captives, even as the slaves in Egypt were freed.*

The children of Israel were being sorely op-
pressed by Pharaoh, and they cried out to the Lord to
deliver them; the merciful Lord heard and delivered
them. In the same way, the children of Adam were
enslaved by the prince of darkness; we called out for
help, and the merciful Lord freed us. God prefigured
this liberation when he delivered Abraham from the
Chaldeans of Ur. The Chaldeans worshiped fire as
a god, but Abraham refused to do so. As a punishment, they threw him into the fire, but the true God
whom he adored delivered him from the flames.[4]
In the same way, God freed his holy ones from the
realm of death. God also prefigured this event by

*Luke 11:21-22

*2 Sam 23:20

*Judg 14:5

[4] This story does not appear in the Bible but circulated in Jewish and Christian circles; Jerome mentions it in his *Hebrew Questions on Genesis* 11:28 (PL 23:956AB).

delivering Lot and his family before the destruction of Sodom: the good were spared, the wicked perished in the firestorm.* In the same way, Christ liberated his saints from limbo, but none of the wicked escaped punishment. The just rejoiced exceedingly, but who can imagine the indescribable bitterness and sorrow of the damned, who dwell forever in eternal flames, palpable darkness, the undying worm, and endless death? Woe to those whose lot it is to experience this calamity, rather than to fear God and believe!

*Gen 19

Christ lingered for a little while in Paradise with the joyful throng. Then he told them that it was time for him to go and take up again his body and awaken it. They all knelt in adoration, asking him to return quickly, because they greatly desired to see his most glorious risen body. *Most gracious Lord, grant that I too may rejoice to see your glorified body when you come again and share with your elect the delight of looking upon you forever.*

As you conclude your meditation on the Lord's passion, ponder all that Jesus endured for our sake, all that he was willing to suffer for our advantage. These words of Jerome can provide a fitting conclusion: "His shame erased our shame; his chains set us free; his crown of thorns won us a royal diadem; by his wounds we were healed; by his burial we rise again; by his descent into hell, we ascend into heaven."*

*Cumm
Mark 14:65;
PL 30:635D

O good Jesus, in your ineffable and loving mercy you would not rest until you had breached the stronghold of death to free those held captive there. Your blessed and most holy soul descended into hell and led out those who dwelled in darkness and the shadow of death. Merciful Jesus, in your loving kindness let your grace and mercy now descend upon the souls of your handmaids and servants, my parents, relatives, friends, and benefactors: deliver them from the punishments they have incurred for their sins, and lead them to eternal joys. Amen.

2

Our Lord's Resurrection

Matt 28:2

Jerome exhorts us,

> Now let us sprinkle the book and the mind's nuptial chamber with fragrant spices in company with the bride and her attendants. Now the king leads us into his storerooms, now the friend Mary arises: *Winter is now past, the rain is over and gone. The flowers have appeared in our land; the voice of the turtledove is heard in our land; the vines in flower yield their sweet smell.* The Bridegroom returns from the shade where he took his midday rest. The bitter root of the cross withers, the flower of life blossoms, heavy with fruit; the one struck down in death rises up in glory; sunrise follows sunset; the eagles gather around the body. After the Sabbath of sorrow a blessed day dawns, the day that holds pride of place: on it light was first created, and on it the Lord rose triumphantly from the dead, exclaiming: *"This is the day which the Lord has made: let us be glad and rejoice in it!"*

*Song 2:11-13

*Ps 117:24;
Cumm Mark
16:1; PL
30:640D

Augustine writes, "After the mockery and the blows, after the wine mixed with vinegar and myrrh, after the agony of crucifixion and the wounds, and, finally, after his descent among the dead, the new flesh arises from his tomb, life returns from hiding in sunset lands, the salvation held onto in death appears again, more glorious after his burial."*

*CA Matt
28:1-7;
Ps-Chrys,
Roland 3.195

Very early on the Lord's Day, the soul of the Lord Jesus, accompanied by a vast retinue of angels, came to the sepulcher. Taking up again his most sacred

10

body, he raised himself from the dead by his own power and left the sealed tomb. No one ever awoke and arose from sleep as effortlessly as Christ arose from death and the tomb. It was for him simply like waking from slumber, as he said himself: *"I have slept and have taken my rest: and I have risen up, because the Lord has protected me."*[*] Bede comments about the hour of Christ's resurrection, "The Lord rose early in the morning from the tomb in which he had been buried in the evening in order to fulfill what was said by the psalmist: *'In the evening weeping shall have place, and in the morning gladness.'"* [*]

*Ps 3:6

*Ps 29:6;
Com Mark
16:8; PL
92:297B

The Angel and the Earthquake

And behold there was a great earthquake at the Lord's resurrection, *for an angel of the Lord descended from heaven* and shook the earth.[*] When Christ died, the earth shook with sorrow; now it trembled with joy. Bede says, "That there was a great earthquake when the Lord rose from the tomb, as there had been when he died on the cross, signifies that hearts that were formerly worldly were to be moved to repentance by faith in his death and resurrection; shaken by salutary fear, they would be lifted up to perpetual life."[*] And Severian asks, "If the earth shook like this when the Lord arose to bring forgiveness to his people, how will it quake with fear when he rises again to punish the wicked? How will it sustain the presence of the Lord when it could not even bear the arrival of an angel?"[*]

*Matt 28:2

*Hom ev
2.1 [2.7]; PL
94:136A

Notice that Scripture describes four earthquakes. The first occurred when the law was given: *The earth was moved, and the heavens dropped at the presence of the God of Sinai, at the presence of the God of Israel.*[*] The second took place during Christ's passion; the third occurred at his resurrection. The fourth earthquake

*Peter
Chrysologus,
Sermo 77; PL
52:418C

*Ps 67:9

will happen at the General Judgment. In a spiritual sense, the earthquake stands for contrition, which is elicited in four different ways: by reflection on the divine commandments, signified by the giving of the law; by meditation on Christ's sorrows and sufferings, symbolized by the passion; by consideration of blessings lost or deferred, suggested by the resurrection; and by thought of the pains of hell, called to mind by the theme of the Last Judgment.

Christ deserved to be raised up by God to the glory of the resurrection because of his filial obedience, for he humbled himself even to death on the cross. Anselm says, "In order to rise up to the glory of his holy resurrection, Christ accepted the mockery of unbelievers, the cruelty of scourges, the humiliation of the cross, the bitterness of gall, and finally death itself. He admonished his followers that if they desired to attain glory after death they should not simply endure with equanimity the toil and difficulties of this life, as well as oppression by wicked people—they must love these things, desire them, and embrace them gratefully."*

*Elmer of Canterbury, Med 1.8 (Anselm Med 1); PL 158:717C

Christ humbled himself for a reason: he embraced evil by dying to deliver us from evil. Then, glorified by rising, he could raise us up to good gifts, as the apostle says: *"He was delivered up for our sins and rose again for our justification."** He underwent his passion to free us from the fires of hell, and he rose from the dead to raise us from death to life. This is why Jesus rightly did not postpone his resurrection later into the third day, so that he rested two nights and one day in the tomb: night pertains to sin, and our nature had experienced a twofold death—the soul's death because of sin and the body's death as a punishment for sin. Because the Lord died only in the body to free us from both bodily and spiritual death, he chose to rest one day and two nights in the grave. The two

*Rom 4:25

nights signify our death in soul and body; the day
signifies his single death, which sheds light on both of
ours. One death he has already destroyed; the second
he will vanquish when he comes again and rewards
the multitude of the elect.[1]

Christ was dead for forty hours to give life to the
four quarters of the earth languishing in death because of the ten commandments of the Law. He rose
on the first day of the week to renew the world on the
same day he had brought it into being. He rose on the
third day of his passion to give life to those who were
dead in sin in three ages: before the Law, under the
Law, and under grace. Augustine suggests that Christ
rose after three days to show that the whole Trinity
assented to the Son's passion. This *triduum* should
be understood symbolically: just as the Trinity first
created humankind in the beginning, so at the end the
whole Trinity restored us through Christ's passion.*

The Lord also hastened his resurrection to put an
end to his disciples' misery. As Pope Leo observes,

*Peter
Chrysologus,
Sermo 72b;
CCL 24A:458

> With wondrous swiftness, the Lord Jesus cut short
> the prophesied period of three days to alleviate
> the troubled spirits of his followers. The last part
> of the first day and the first part of the third day
> were conjoined to the second full day so that the
> span of time was shortened without the number
> of days being reduced. Our Savior's resurrection
> did not allow his soul to tarry long in the under-
> world or his flesh in the tomb; so quickly was his
> uncorrupted body restored to life that it seemed
> more like sleep than death. Divinity, which did
> not withdraw from either the soul or the body of
> the human nature the Son had assumed, joined
> by its power what it had divided by its power.*

*Sermo 71.2;
PL 54:387D

[1] The theme of our twofold death and Christ's single death is
found in Augustine, De Trin 4.13.17 (PL 42:899).

Christ gives us a twofold example in his passion and resurrection: in his passion, a model of patience; in his resurrection, a cause for hope. He shows us two aspects of our earthly life—toil, which we should endure, and blessedness, for which we should hope.

Christ's Glorified Body

Christ rose with a glorified body. His soul was glorious from the first moment of his conception, on account of the clear vision and perfect enjoyment of his divine nature. But by divine dispensation the soul's glory was not shared with his body, so that it would be mortal and able to suffer, for in this way Christ could pay our debt and accomplish the plan of redemption. When the mystery of the passion was completed and Christ's soul was reunited with his body, he immediately imparted this glory to his body. Augustine says, "He bore the infirmity of the flesh, but this infirmity was swallowed up by his resurrection."* And Leo writes,

*Tr John ev 60.5; PL 35:1799

> As the apostle teaches, *"And if we have known Christ according to the flesh, now we know him so no longer."** The resurrection did not put an end to Christ's flesh: it changed it; its substance was not destroyed, but its power was increased. Its quality changed; its nature did not pass away. It was rightly said that the flesh of Christ became unknown in the condition in which it had been known, because nothing remained that was capable of suffering, nothing remained that was weak. His body is the same in its nature, but it is not the same in its glory.*

*2 Cor 5:16

*Sermo 71.4; PL 54:388C

At this time, O my soul, let us abandon devout lamentations, dispel the clouds of sorrow, and breathe in the serene air of holy joy. We have shed tears at the burial of the Redeemer, who *by dying destroyed our death*; now let us celebrate the glory and resurrection of him who *by rising restored our life.* As the apostle teaches, *Christ, rising again from the dead, dies now no more. Death shall no more have dominion over him.* God the Father has clothed him with the garment of immortality and glory and placed upon his head the victor's crown, lavishing upon him all the wondrous treasures of heaven.

*Roman Missal, Easter Preface
*Rom 6:9

All joy, happiness, and exultation are full to overflowing in the risen Christ. His flesh, the most beautiful flower from the root of Jesse, had blossomed at birth, springing up as a singularly lovely bloom from the sinless Virgin. That flower withered in the passion, when no beauty or comeliness could be found in it. But now, having recovered the blood poured out on the cross, it blossoms anew in glory, with all the splendid qualities of true human nature. It is robed in such wondrous splendor that it outshines the sun itself! Christ's glorified body offers an example of the beauty that will be enjoyed by all the elect, as he himself described it: *Then shall the just shine as the sun, in the kingdom of their Father,* that is, in eternal beatitude. If the just will shine as the sun, who can imagine the splendor of the Sun of Justice himself? It eclipses the sun's brightness and does not take second place to all the constellations of the stars.

*Matt 13:43

Then Christ's youth was renewed like an eagle's, then the lion roused his whelp, then the Phoenix was reborn, then the spoiled vessel was reworked into one more pleasing to the eye, then Jonah emerged unharmed from the whale,† then the candelabrum of pure gold was fashioned,** then the fallen tent of David was raised up again,** then the sun that had been hidden by clouds shone,†† then the dead grain of wheat cast into the earth germinated, then the stag grew new antlers, then Samson pulled up the city's gates and escaped, then Joseph was led out of prison

*Ps 102:5
*Gen 49:9
*Ambrose, Hex 5.23.79; PL 14:238B
*Jer 18:4
†Jonah 2:11
**Exod 37:17
**Amos 9:11
††2 Macc 1:22
*John 12:25

*Judg 16:3

°Gen 41:39
°Ps 29:12

to become ruler in Egypt,° then the loosed sackcloth
was girded with joy.° [2]

Easter, the Solemnity of Solemnities

Our Easter celebration surpasses all other feasts
in solemnity; each Sunday is like an octave of Easter,
marked with every expression of joy. The nobility of
the Lord's Day is well known: it is the first of days,
with no night preceding it; it is also the last of days,
with no night following. On this day the heavens
and the earth were made, on this day the angels were
created and turned to God, on this day the Law was
given to the children of Israel, on this day Christ was
born and on this day he rose from the dead, on this
day the Holy Spirit was given to the apostles, on this
day we will all rise and be judged, on this day the
praise of God resounds that will last for all eternity.
As Gregory the Great says,

> I am right in speaking about the nobility of the
> Easter solemnity, because it surpasses all others.
> In sacred speech it is customary to underscore
> the excellence of something by saying "the Holy
> of Holies" or "The Song of Songs"; so Easter can
> rightly be called the Solemnity of Solemnities. On
> this feast the pattern of our own resurrection is
> given, the hope of reaching our heavenly home-
> land is enkindled, and we experience by antici-

---

[2] It was believed that the lion was asleep at birth, and on the third
day its father's roar awakened it (Isidore, Ety 12.2.5; PL 82:434B).
The mythical bird that rose to new life every five hundred years
from the ashes of its own pyre was taken to be symbolic of Christ's
resurrection from the earliest days of Christianity (see Clement
of Rome, Letter, chap. 25; Tertullian, De res carnis, chap. 13; PL
2:811B). According to medieval lore, the stag could kill poisonous
serpents with its breath (see Isidore, Ety 12.1.18; PL 82:427A). To
counteract the snake's venom, the stag drank large amounts of
water and then shed and regrew its antlers.

pation the glory of the supernal realm. By this
solemnity the elect, slumbering in undisturbed
rest within the confines of the lower world, were
led back to the pleasant places of Paradise. What
is this solemnity? It has shattered the prison of the
netherworld and opened the gates of the kingdom
of heaven.*

*40 hom 22.6;
PL 76:177B

Here is Augustine's praise of this feast:

This cheerful day shines, not with the light of the
sun in its orbit, but with the more sublime splendor of the Lamb risen from the dead. On this day
Christ, the Sun of Justice, arose from the realm of
death, and so we pluck David's harp and sing,
*"This is the day which the Lord has made: let us be
glad and rejoice in it."* * Let us contemplate this day
and ponder the night that gave birth to it. This
night, which reproduces the starry firmament;
this night, in which heaven and earth rejoice;
this night, pregnant with blessings; this night, of
which it is said, *"Night shall be light all the day"* *
and from which is born *the day which the Lord has
made*, the Lord's Day. Rightly has this been called
the *dies lucis*, for on it the dark clouds of blindness
were scattered. Those *that sat in the region of the
shadow of death* exclaimed, *"Light is sprung up!"* *
   Let the earth rejoice, for she sees a new light; let
the angels rejoice, for the Lord lavishes glory on
sinners. The inferno shook from sustaining such
matchless splendor; every knee bent to Christ the
Lord, in the heavens, on the earth, and under the
earth. All creation triumphs with us, and angels,
archangels, and every order of blessed spirits
join in our joyful feast. We for our part rely on
those celestial choirs to bolster our refrain, for our
human tongues fall far short of giving God due
praise. Let us then rejoice in the Lord, but with
reverent awe, not careless abandon. Saint John
the Forerunner leaped in his mother's womb,
but heeding the command of Gabriel he never

*Ps 117:24

*Ps 138:12

*Matt 4:16

drank wine. Weak as we are, let us drink soberly, avoiding excess. In this way our festive rejoicing will not stir up unworthy feelings; rather, we will enter salvation's harbor with temperate serenity. Let us grasp the prize of fasting so that the victory feast will not slip through our fingers, that celebration the Lord helps us attain. He conquered for us by suffering, so that we could worthily sing the paean, *"Death is swallowed up in victory, alleluia!"* *

*1 Cor 15:54;
Caillau 67;
Ps-Aug,
Sermo 55,
approx

On this day Christ, accompanied by the thief, did what no one else could do: he extinguished the fiery sword guarding the gates of Paradise and entered in, saying to the angels, *"Open to me the gates of justice: I will go in to them, and give praise to the Lord."* * Since the Lord's passion this gate has been both closed and open: closed to sinners and unbelievers, open to the just and to believers. Just as the Virgin Mary, the Mother of the Lord, holds first place among women, so this is the mother of all other days. This day is one of the seven, but is also outside the seven; it is called "the eighth day," for which reason a few psalms are given the title *pro octava*. On this day the Synagogue ends and the Church is born. On this day eight souls were saved in Noah's ark.

*Ps 117:19

How can I go on? Should I wish to mention all the mysteries connected with this day, the day itself would not be long enough! This I will add: the ancient observance of the Jewish Sabbath was ordained for the sake of this solemnity, the universal Sabbath of grace. The Jews did not carry out any servile labor on the Sabbath; we do not work on the Lord's Day, because it is the day of resurrection. They did not venture from their homes on the Sabbath; we do not leave the Lord's house on Sunday. They did not kindle a fire on the Sabbath, but we on the contrary do kindle within ourselves the fire of the Holy Spirit, that fire about which the Lord said, *"I am come to cast fire on the earth. And what will I, but that it be kindled?"* * How the Lord

*Luke 12:49

wants this fire to be kindled in us, so that by the
warmth of the Holy Spirit the love of God will
not grow cold! The Israelites sacrificed a lamb or
a kid; Christ is slain for us. For all of these reasons,
brothers and sisters, we join together and sing
with one voice, *"This is the day which the Lord has
made: let us be glad and rejoice in it."* ˙

˙Maximus
of Turin,
Sermo 28,
approx; PL
57:905B–906D

Concerning the exclamation *Alleluia*! that is customarily used throughout the Easter season, the same
Augustine has this to say:

Therefore, let us sing from here *Alleluia*, which
means "Praise the Lord!" Let us sing to the Lord,
brothers and sisters, with our lives and tongues,
with our hearts and lips, with our voices and our
deeds. God wants us to sing *alleluia* to him in such
a way that our conduct does not contradict our
praise. O, the blessed *alleluia* of heaven, where the
angels form God's temple! The singers enjoy the
greatest interior harmony there, where no law in
the members is at odds with the law of the mind,
where no swaggering ambition threatens the triumph of charity.

Let us here sing *alleluia* even in our anxiety, so
that later we can sing it there in security,˙ when
temptation has been left behind and this mortal
body has put on immortality and incorruptibility. O, the joy of the heavenly *alleluia*, sung in a
life free from care, in fear of no adversary! There
we shall make no enemies and lose no friends.
God's praises are sung both here and hereafter:
here in anxiety, there in security; here by those
who must die, there by those who will live forever; here in hope, there in fulfillment; here on
pilgrimage, there at home. So, my friends, let us
sing here to lighten our labors, not to pass a life
of leisure. Sing as travelers do—sing, but keep
walking, sing to alleviate the tedium. Don't be
lazy: walk and advance in doing good. Sing and

˙Sermo
256.1–3; PL
38:1190–91

*Sermo 256.3;
PL 38:1193
walk: don't wander from the road; don't retrace
your steps; don't lag behind.*

And Bede writes,

> After all our trials have ceased, our life will be
> taken up entirely with God's praises. Therefore it
> is our custom to commemorate this peaceful and
> blissful state by chanting *alleluia* more frequently
> and joyfully during these fifty days. . . . In the
> book of Revelation, John the Evangelist says that
> he heard the throngs of heavenly powers sing-
> ing this word.* And the venerable father Tobit,
> perceiving something of the glory of the citizens
> on high and the splendor of the heavenly Jerusa-
> lem, described it with these mystical words: *All
> its streets shall be paved with white and clean stones,
> and Alleluia shall be sung in its streets.**

*Rev 19:1

*Tob 13:22
(Vlg); Hom
Ev 2.10; PL
94:185A

Arise now with Christ, my soul, from the fetid
tomb of your sins, and breathe in the hope of resurrection and eternal life. Die in this life for the love
of God, so that after the resurrection you may enjoy
the life to come. If we bear bodily death now out of
love for Christ, we shall reign with him later in joy.
Let us make it our business to enter into the earthly
celebration in such a way that we may deserve to take
part in the angelic one. Gregory urges us,

> We have completed the paschal solemnities; but
> by our lives we must become worthy to arrive
> at the eternal feast. All earthly feasts come to an
> end. Take care that you celebrate the paschal feast
> in time in such a way that you do not exclude
> yourself from the eternal solemnity. What does
> it profit you to participate in human ceremonies
> if you absent yourself from those of the angels?
> This present feast is only a shadow of the feast to
> come. We take part in the annual Easter feast so
> that we may be brought to the Easter that has no

end. The observance of Easter at its appointed
time increases our yearning for the feast to come.
Our attendance at this passing solemnity should
inflame our hearts to long for eternal joys. Then
we will enjoy perfectly and with true happiness in
our homeland what we contemplate in shadows
on our pilgrimage.*

*40 hom
26.10; PL
76:1202D

Christ's resurrection was prefigured by the
mighty Samson, who entered the city of his enemies
and passed the night there. His foes kept watch at the
city gates so that they could seize him in the morning
and kill him—but he awoke at midnight and, pulling
up the very gates of the city, carried them off.* In like
manner, Christ entered with power into the citadel of
his enemy, the realm of death, and, having destroyed
it, arose in the middle of the night. His resurrection
was also prefigured by Jonah, who was kept alive for
three days in the belly of the whale and after three
days emerged alive on dry land.*

*Judg 16:2-3

*Jonah 2

Christ's resurrection was also prefigured by the
stone rejected by the builders of the temple. The stone
was thrown away because they thought it was use-
less. But when it came time to complete the construc-
tion of the temple and they needed a cornerstone
to connect the two walls, the only one that fit was
the very stone they had discarded. Christ was the
stone rejected in his passion, but after his resurrection he became the cornerstone of the church. Thus
was fulfilled the prophecy of David: *The stone which
the builders rejected, the same is become the head of the
corner*—and so this psalm is sung at the feast of his
resurrection.* This stone joins together the two walls
of the Lord's temple because Christ built his one
church from two peoples, the Jews and the Gentiles.
In this spiritual temple the cement is his blood and
the stones are his most sacred body.

*Ps 117:22

Lord Jesus Christ, so singularly pleasing, having broken the chains of death you glorified your body and arose from the dead with ineffable splendor. Grant, I beseech you, that by your life-giving resurrection I may rise from my sins and spiritual death, and always produce the flowers of virtue. May I continually walk in newness of life, seeking and knowing the things that are above rather than those of earth. By the power of your luminous glory expel the darkness of sin from my soul, so that on the day of universal resurrection my body may rise into glory and I, body and soul, may rejoice with you eternally. Amen.

3

The Myrrh-Bearing Women; Jesus Appears to His Mother

At about the same time that Jesus rose—that is, very early in the morning—Mary Magdalen, Mary the mother of James the Less, Mary the mother of Zebedee's sons, and some other women were moved by their faith and devotion for the Lord to ask leave of our Lady to bring aromatic spices to Jesus' tomb in order to anoint his body. She remained at home, weeping and praying. How beautiful it is that these women all answered to the same name: it is fitting that those animated by a common desire also shared a common name. Reflect that there are three ways of life among those who seek Christ, and no one can be saved apart from these: the penitent (beginners), the proficient (followers of the active life), and the perfect (contemplatives). These three states are symbolized by the three Marys who went in search of the Lord.

The Three Marys: Penitent, Proficient, Perfect

Penitents are represented by Mary Magdalen, a disreputable sinner who repented. True, she also symbolizes the contemplative life, but the evangelist Mark describes her as *Mary Magdalen, out of whom he had cast seven devils*, so she is numbered among the penitents, and indeed the gospel presents her as the foremost example of repentance.* The name *Mary* is appropriate for her when it is interpreted as *bitter sea* (*mare amarum*) according to the Latin etymology, or from the Hebrew word *mara*, which is

*Mark 16:9

23

"bitter" in Latin. Hence we read in the book of Ruth, *Call me not Noemi (that is, beautiful), but call me Mara (that is, bitter), for the Almighty has quite filled me with bitterness.* This meaning of the name is confirmed in Mary Magdalen's case when we see her prostrate at Jesus' feet, washing away the stains of her sins with her tears.*[1]

*Ruth 1:20

*Luke 7:38

The proficient, or those in the active life, are represented by Mary of Cleophas, the mother of James; these disciples struggle to overcome vice and grow in virtue. Another meaning of *Mary* is appropriate for them: in Syriac, the name is interpreted as *Domina.* Those who are making progress struggle because of the attraction of sin and the difficulty of doing good. They must dominate their passions with reason so as not to give into temptation. Virtue comes from this battle against sensuality: *Power* is made perfect in infirmity.* The perfect, or contemplatives, are represented by Mary of Salome, the mother of Zebedee's sons, James the Greater and John. She asked for a kingdom for her sons. Contemplatives concern themselves only with the kingdom of God; it is already within them to some extent, and they enjoy a foretaste of the kingdom of heaven. The name *Salome* means *peaceful,* and in this life the only true peace is found in contemplation. This resonates with a third meaning of the name *Mary,* that is, *illuminata.* The contemplative soul responds to the invitation of the prophet Isaiah: *Arise, be enlightened, O Jerusalem: for your light is come, and the glory of the Lord is risen upon you.*

*virtus

*2 Cor 12:19

*Isa 60:1

Each of these Marys carries spices and ointments symbolic of her vocation. In a moral sense, these three women can be taken to represent the just person's

---

[1] Western tradition at least as far back as Gregory the Great held the sinful woman in Luke 7, Mary of Bethany, and Mary Magdalen to be the same person.

mind, tongue, and hands; each of these has its own very precious ointments. The ointments of the mind are contrition, compassion, and devotion. Contrition is made from the rank weeds growing in our own garden, that is, our sins; compassion is made from the bitter plants growing in other people's gardens, that is, our neighbors' misfortunes; devotion is made from the precious plants obtained from the Lord's garden, that is, Christ's blessings. The ointments of the tongue are heartfelt prayer, thorough confession of sins, and proclamation of the truth. Prayer is made from a mixture of the herbs of right intention, firm attention, and devout affection; confession is blended from shame for sins committed, regret for sins of omission, and fear of punishment; true preaching is formulated from the spices of doctrinal instruction, moral exhortation, and the correction of vices. The ointments of the hands are the seven corporal works of mercy, which are summed up in this verse: *Colligo, poto, cibo, redimo, tego, visito, condo.*[2] Whoever wants to have these spices and ointments must purchase them. When people buy, they give something of their own and receive something from another; here, in order to perform virtuous works we must give something of our own (our will) in order to obtain something from God (the ability to do what must be done).

Several other women were also Jesus' followers, but these three made a special effort to go to his tomb because they felt a deeper obligation to him, for he had bestowed many blessings on them. Mary Magdalen felt a singular attachment to Christ because

[2] The traditional list of these works is to feed the hungry (*cibo*), to give drink to the thirsty (*poto*), to clothe the naked (*colligo*), to ransom the imprisoned (*redimo*), to shelter the homeless (*tego*), to visit the sick (*visito*), and to bury the dead (*condo*). The source of the summary verse is unknown.

he had cast seven demons out of her. Mary of James
and Mary of Salome had special ties to Jesus because
he was their nephew and he had made their sons
apostles.[3]

Christ Appears to His Mother

It may seem surprising that the Blessed Virgin
chose to remain at home and did not accompany
these women to the tomb. Three explanations can
be given for this. First, it is likely that she could not
see her son's burial place without experiencing profound grief, especially because the recollection of
his horrible death was still so fresh. The sight of his
tomb would have pierced her heart with a sword of
sorrow. Secondly, she was so completely exhausted
from her weeping and mourning on Friday and Saturday that she could barely stand. Augustine says,
"That loving mother was so overwhelmed with sorrow and so exhausted with suffering that she was
beside herself and had hardly been able to bear being
present at Christ's burial."* The third reason is that
the other women thought that Christ's body was still
in the tomb, and, following the ancient custom, they
wanted to anoint the corpse to preserve it from rot-
ting, worms, and decomposition.

*Ps-Aug
Sermo 1 de
res; Liverani
23

But they were mistaken. Christ's body was em-
balmed by its divinity: it could lie in the ground for
ten thousand years and would not putrefy, be prey to
worms, or turn to dust. The Blessed Virgin, however,
knew that her son's body was not there because he

[3] According to a medieval legend, Saint Ann had three husbands
and a daughter from each named Mary: Mary, the mother of Jesus;
Mary of Cleophas, the mother of James the Less, Simon, and Jude;
and Mary of Salome, the mother of James the Greater and John.
The earliest mention is found in the writings of the 9th-c. Haymo
of Auxerre (PL 118:823–24).

had already risen, immortal and incorruptible; so even if she could have visited the tomb, she did not wish to. As she kept vigil and fasted in her grief, Mary remembered her son shackled, flogged, and nailed to the cross and struck her breast with her delicate hand. Worn out in body and spirit, she sat in a room by herself, weeping and lamenting over the calamities that had befallen them.

As our Lady was praying and quietly shedding tears, suddenly the Lord Jesus came, clothed in brilliant white robes of glory, in the freshness of his resurrection. With a serene countenance, he appeared completely festive to his mournful mother—beautiful, glorious, and joyful. At the sight of her son, Mary stood up, adored him, and embraced him in tears; all her bitterness was turned to joy! Then they sat together, and she carefully scrutinized his face and every wound visible on his body, solicitously asking if all his pain and sorrow had truly been banished. O, what joy filled his mother as she looked at the son who from now on could never suffer again! Not only would he live forever, but he was the undisputed ruler of every creature in heaven and on earth. They remained together for some time, conversing lovingly and joyfully about this remarkable Passover. The Lord Jesus told his mother how he had passed these three days, and how he had freed his people from the realm of death. This was truly the great paschal feast!

There is no mention made in the gospels of this meeting between the risen Jesus and his mother before he appeared to the others, but I have chosen to include it here before describing those encounters because it may devoutly be believed, and it is fully described in a certain *Legend of the Resurrection*. It was certainly fitting that before appearing to anyone else the risen Christ should first visit his mother to share with her the joy of his resurrection, because her love for him was deeper than the others'. And, because of this love, she had suffered more than anyone else during his passion and so looked forward more eagerly to his resurrection. Although the gospels say nothing about this event, it may certainly be piously believed.[4]

What does it matter that the gospels do not speak of this incident? As John the Evangelist tells us, not everything Jesus did was written down. It is not reasonable to insist that this meeting never took place because the evangelists provide no details about where and how it happened. Could such a son so grievously neglect such a mother—he who had commanded us to honor our father and our mother? It may be that the evangelists pass over this in silence because their purpose is to produce witnesses to the fact of Christ's resurrection, and it would not be seemly to call the mother to give evidence for her son. If those who heard what the other women reported thought them crazy, how much more would they dismiss the words spoken in honor of the son by his mother! So the evangelists chose not to record the event in writing, but it was handed on as something well known. Ambrose says, "Mary saw the Lord's resurrection; she was the first to see, and she believed. Mary Magdalen saw, although she still wavered."[*] And Anselm writes,

*De vir 3.16; PL 16:270A

> If someone should ask me why the evangelists do not describe the most loving risen Lord appearing first to his most dear mother to lessen her sorrow, I would give the answer I heard from a very

---

[4]Ludolph is quoting from a *Commentary on St. Matthew* by Bruno of Segni (PL 165:310C). It is not clear what work he is referring to in the *Legenda de Resurrectione*. Apocryphal works, referred to by writers as early as Origen and Jerome, present accounts of the risen Christ appearing to his mother at his tomb.

learned man about this. He said, "The authority
of the evangelists is so solemn that they recorded
only what was essential, and there is nothing superfluous or unnecessary in their accounts. If they
had written that after rising from the dead the son
himself had appeared to his mother, the queen of
the world, as he did to others, would such a report
not be superfluous? Would this not seem to put
the queen of heaven and earth on the same level
as the other men and women to whom Christ appeared? His Spirit had rested fully and perfectly
in her and had revealed to her all that Jesus was
and did with penetrating clarity, and the evangelists recorded that this or that happened in such
and such a way as she told them.'"

*Eadmer,
de exc 6; PL
159:568B

Sedulius writes in his Easter poem, "She remains
ever a virgin, to whom the Lord first showed himself
at dawn.'" When we read that Jesus appeared *first
to Mary Magdalen,* it should be interpreted to mean
first among those who were to bear witness to his
resurrection; he appeared first to his Virgin mother,
not so that she could testify to his resurrection, but
to give her the joy of seeing him.

*Sedulius
5.361; PL
19:743A
*Mark 16:9

> *O Mary, Mother of God and Virgin full of grace, you
> are the solace of all the forsaken who call out to you.
> By virtue of the great joy that consoled you when you
> knew that the Lord Jesus had risen from the dead on
> the third day, never to die again, be now the comforter
> of my soul. May you also deign to help me on the last
> day, when I will be raised up body and soul and called
> to give an account before your only-begotten Son for
> my every deed and thought. Loving Virgin Mother,
> help me to escape the sentence of eternal damnation
> and arrive at eternal joys with all God's elect. Amen.*

4

The Disciples at the Empty Tomb

Matt 28:1-8; Mark 16:1-8; Luke 24:1-12; John 20:1-10

And in the end of the night following *the Sabbath,*

·Matt 28:1 *when it began to dawn toward the first day of the week,·* which we call the Lord's Day, *very early in the morn-*

·Mark 16:2 *ing, the sun being now risen·* (that is, at that twilight hour when the sun has not yet appeared above the horizon, but the eastern sky is brightened by its approach), the three *Marys came to the sepulcher, bringing*

·Luke 24:1 *the spices which they had prepared.·*

The women came so early that, in John's words,

·John 20:1 *it was yet dark;·* according to Luke, they came *very early in the morning,* in the twilight between darkness

·Luke 24:1 and the full light of day that we call dawn.· Mark

·Mark 16:2 for his part says *very early, the sun being now risen.·* These differences can be explained in the literal sense by saying that the women started out when it was still dark, walked to the tomb during the twilight, and arrived as the sun was rising. But we can read a symbolic meaning into these diverse terms when we recall that these women represent three ways of discipleship: darkness standing for beginners, dawn for the proficient, and sunrise for the perfect. Christians should seek Christ *early*, not giving in to laziness; they should seek him *the first day after the Sabbath*, that is, with tranquility and a Sabbath peace of heart, not in discord and agitation; and they should *come to the tomb* and seek the Lord there.

The tomb represents the human soul at each stage: the heart of the penitent is likened to a tomb on account of sorrow, for just as mourners gather around a grave, so penitents weep over their sins; the heart of the proficient is likened to a tomb on account of works of mercy, such as burying the dead and other charitable acts; the heart of the contemplative is likened to a tomb on account of repose, for as it is said that the dead rest in their graves, so great inner stillness is the hallmark of the contemplative life.

So Christians of every kind do well to seek Christ in the tomb of the heart. But it is necessary to remove the large stone obstructing the entrance to the sepulcher, as the angel did on Easter morning, as we will soon see. Every stage has its own large stone that prevents us from entering into the depths of the heart and that must be removed with effort. For penitents, the obstacle is the attraction of sin; for the proficient, it is the difficulty of doing good; for contemplatives, it is the attraction of visible things. The obstacle can be completely taken away at every stage by the grace of the Holy Spirit if a soul devoutly seeks this alone.

Blessed is that Mary, the soul, who comes to see Christ's tomb by meditation, weeps there from compassion, and anoints him by devotion! Let us imitate these holy women. They came to the sepulcher, the resting place of the dead, seeking the Lord with the spices of heartfelt love and devotion. Let us set out carrying our ointments—good works, fragrant virtue, sweet prayer—and go in search of God with all our desires. Let us look for him not in the grave but in heaven, where we know he has ascended. Gregory the Great says, "The holy women who had followed the Lord came with spices to the tomb; they had loved him when he was alive, and they wanted to lavish their affection on him in death. We who believe in him who died certainly approach his tomb with spices if we are strengthened by the fragrance of virtue and seek him by carrying out works of mercy."*

*40 hom 21.2;
PL 76:1170C

In a spiritual sense, the tomb also symbolizes the Body and Blood of Christ, which should only be approached *after the Sabbath,* in peace and tranquility of heart; *very early in the morning,* with the fervor of urgent desire; at *dawn,* when the darkness of sin is scattered by the rising sun of grace; and *bringing the spices* of charitable deeds and a good reputation. Those who do not approach the Eucharist in this way should be on guard lest they eat and drink their own judgment. Bede writes, "That the holy women came to the tomb *very early in the morning* means, in the literal sense, the great fervor of charity they showed in seeking and finding the Lord. In a spiritual sense, however, it instructs us on how we should approach the most holy Body of Christ—with our faces illumined and the darkness of sin scattered. His holy sepulcher is a symbol of the Lord's altar, upon which the mysteries of his Body and Blood are celebrated. The spices carried by the women signify the fragrance of virtue and sweet perfume of prayer with which we should approach the altar."*

*Com Luke 24:1; PL 92:623A

It is fitting that the church celebrates Lauds early in the morning in memory of the Lord's resurrection. Peter Comestor gives this explanation: "By *very early in the morning* the evangelist means *dawn.* Dawn is the interval between the darkness of night and the full light of day, during which the joyful approach of the world's salvation must be proclaimed in the church, just as the sun tints the sky in advance of its rising. This presage allows her to adjust her eyes to the splendor of the Lord's resurrection when it dawns. At that hour the whole church imitates the holy women and sings the praises of Christ, whose resurrection refreshes us by giving us confidence and bathing us in the light of belief."*

*Hist ev 185; PL 198:1636D– 1637C

When the women had passed the city gates on their way to the tomb, they remembered all the mis-

ery and affliction their Lord and Teacher had suffered,
and, at each of the places associated with these sad
events, they stopped, knelt, and kissed the ground.
Groaning and sighing deeply, they said, "Here is
where we met him bearing the cross on his shoul-
der, and it seemed his mother would die from grief."
"There is where he turned to talk to the women."
"That is where he dropped the cross from exhaustion—and there is the stone he stumbled over." "This
is where they cruelly goaded him on, forcing him
almost to run." "Here is where they stripped him of
his clothing and nailed him to the cross." Then, their
eyes streaming with tears, they fell to their faces on
the ground to adore that cross, reddened with his
precious blood, and reverently kissed it.

Getting up again, and heading toward the sepulcher, they remembered the large stone that had
been placed over its entrance. It was so huge that it
had required twenty strong men to move it, and they
were just three women. They said to one another,
*"Who shall roll us back the stone from the door of the
sepulcher* so that we can enter?"* In other words, "We
cannot remove it by ourselves, *for it was very great."**
But although they said these things, they did not turn
back, confident that with the Lord what seems to be
beyond human strength is possible.

*Mark 16:3
*Mark 16:4

Angels at the Tomb

And looking, they saw the stone rolled back by an
angel who, presenting himself to worship his Lord,
had come to show that Christ's resurrection had already taken place. This very angel of the Lord was
sitting on the stone outside the tomb. The sepulcher
can be understood to represent the Scriptures, in
which the Lord had been interred under a multitude of figures, but after the resurrection, the Angel

*Mark 16:4

of Great Counsel has brought to light all difficulties.
Bede suggests that rolling away the stone signifies
the revelation of the sacraments of Christ, which lay
hidden under the letter of the legal observance; the
law was carved in stone, and so it is represented by
the stone.*

*Com Mark
16:4; PL
92:295B

In a moral sense this stone signifies the burden of
penitence that makes some people lose heart when
they begin their conversion, because they are not sure
they can complete the penance they have begun. With
great anxiety they ask, *"Who shall roll us back the stone
from the door of the sepulcher*, that is, from the heart in
which Christ desires to be buried?" But they should
not hesitate or turn back; rather, let them walk hand
in hand with these women. The grace of the Holy
Spirit will descend like an angel from heaven to roll
away the stone, lifting up the whole burden of penance. The Lord himself said, *"My yoke is sweet and my
burden light"* when divine grace helps.

*Matt 11:30

*And entering into the sepulcher, they saw a young
man sitting on the right side, clothed with a white robe;
and they were astonished* with joy and wonder at such
a vision. The angel had the appearance and garb of
a youth, on account of the surpassing immortality
of resurrection life, which restores our youth like an
eagle's and in which no one grows old. Gregory says,
"He sat to the right in a white robe because he was
announcing the joy of the festive day for both men
and angels. The Lord's resurrection led us back to
immortality, but it also repaired the losses sustained
in heaven by the defection of the wicked angels."*
The angel's white robe suggests the purity of life that
a person should observe after baptism. Two angels
were seen, one at the entrance and a second inside
the tomb, so that there would be the required number
of witnesses: *In the mouth of two or three witnesses shall
every word stand.*

*Mark 16:5

*40 hom 21.2;
PL 76:1171A

*2 Cor 13:1

The earth had quaked when the Lord rose, but he left the tomb before the stone was rolled away, just as a little later he would pass through closed doors to be with his disciples. After the resurrection, the angel moved the stone when he descended to show that the sepulcher was empty because the risen Lord had left the tomb. He who had broken down the gates of hell by his own power needed no angelic help in his resurrection. Chrysostom asks, "For whose sake did the angel come and remove the stone after the resurrection? It was done for the women. They saw the angel inside the tomb; he had taken the stone away so that the women could see that the body was not there and believe that Christ had risen."* Gregory says that the women carrying the spices saw the angels because those whose holy desires lead them toward God, accompanied by fragrant virtues, be-
hold spiritually the citizens of heaven.*

    The angel is described as having a countenance like lightning and brilliant white vesture, so that his mien terrified the wicked and his robes helped the good to believe in Christ's resurrection—for awe and love lead to faith. *His countenance was as lightning*, for his face appeared to be aflame, causing terror in the guards, *and his raiment as snow,* giving comfort to the women. Lightning denotes the panic caused by fear, but the white robes proclaim the joy of the Lord's res-
urrection. This is why white vestments are worn for the liturgy during the Easter season. The evangelist adds, *"and for fear of him* and his face, which looked like lightning, *the guards were struck with terror* and im-
mediately fell to the ground like dead men." See how stern he appeared, and how he terrified the wicked! And so Rabanus Maurus observes, *"They were struck with terror* and anxious fear because they did not have loving faith; *and they became as dead men* because they refused to accept the truth of the resurrection."* Here

*Hom John 85.4; PG 59:464

*40 hom 21.21; PL 76:1170C

*Matt 28:3

*Matt 28:4

*CA Matt 28:1-7

we see how to distinguish a good spirit from an evil one, right from the outset. A good angel first frightens with his brilliance, then he comforts with his words; finally, he gives joy with the consolation he sends. An evil spirit does the opposite: first he frightens with his horrible voice, then he deceives with false promises; finally, he brings sadness with the deception he has achieved.

And the angel answering the trepidation of the women *said to them: "Fear not."** Gregory suggests that this was as much as to say, "Let those be frightened who do not love the arrival of heavenly residents; let those tremble who, weighed down by earthly desires, despair at being able to attain fellowship with them. But you, why do you shrink from your fellow citizens, the servants of the one you are seeking? See how he coaxes those who are good and appears gentle to them."*

The angel went on, *"I know that you seek* in his tomb *Jesus* the Savior *who was crucified,* as if he were dead."* He said *who was crucified* to recall the benefits of his passion, as the apostle says, *"Think diligently upon him that endured such opposition from sinners against himself,"** and to praise the women for seeking Jesus crucified. Many people seek Jesus the Savior, but not Jesus crucified, that is, on his cross, although he will be found nowhere but there. Chrysostom says, "Many gladly seek him robed in royal purple, few seek him whipped or crucified; but before he can be found arrayed in purple, he must be sought scourged."*

Then the angel said, *"He is not here* in his bodily, carnal presence (although he is nowhere absent in his majestic divinity). *For he is risen* in his humanity, he who could in no way suffer in his divinity." He added *"as he said"* to remind them of Christ's words before his passion; this would strengthen their con-

*Matt 28:5

*40 hom 21.3;
PL 76:1171B

*Matt 28:5

*Heb 12:3

*Source
unknown

viction that he had already risen, since it is impossible that something could not happen when he said
it would. Then he showed them the tomb and said,
"Come, and see the place where the Lord was laid." * It
is as if the angel said, "Do you want proof of his
resurrection? *See the place where they laid him.* If you
do not believe my words, look at the empty tomb
and believe the testimony of your eyes." And this
was why he had rolled back the stone—so that they
could see the place. Although the faithful throughout
the world sing, "The Lord is risen from the tomb; he
hung upon the tree for us," only the canons of the
Church of the Resurrection in Jerusalem enjoy the
privilege of proclaiming, "The Lord is risen from the
tomb," with the evidence of it before their very eyes.
Similarly, when the deacon there reads the words in
the Easter gospel, *"He is risen, he is not here,"* he points
to the Holy Sepulcher.

*Matt 28:6

Then the angel said, *"But go* quickly, *tell his disciples and Peter that he goes before you into Galilee. There
you shall see him, as he told you** before his passion, so
that you can follow him there."* It was as if he said,
"Do not keep this great joy of yours locked up in
your hearts. Share it with the other lovers, those who
are Christ's disciples, not lovers of the world." *There
you shall see him*, in a place nearby, and soon. He goes
before you *into Galilee*, because the place that saw the
beginnings of the splendor of grace will also be the
place to behold the beginnings of glory. The Lord
wished particularly to appear in Galilee to demonstrate the truth of his resurrection, because he had
performed many miracles there and had preached
much there, and so he was better known there.

*Mark 16:7

The angel specifically said *and Peter* because of his
preeminence among the disciples, so that he would
not despair of being pardoned because of the enor-
mity of his sin of apostasy, and so that he would not

avoid the presence of the Lord he had denied or fear
to join the other disciples. For, as Jerome says, Peter
felt he was no longer worthy to be a disciple because
he had three times denied his Master.˙ And Gregory
writes, "If this angel had not mentioned by name the
man who had denied his master, he would not have
dared to join the disciples. He was called by name,
so that he would not despair because of his denial."˙
For, as Jerome observes, past sins do no harm when
they cause no pleasure.˙

Now let us consider a question raised by Augustine: why did the angel, at the Lord's direction, say
he goes before you into Galilee, implying that this would
be Christ's only appearance or that it would happen
soon, when in fact it did not happen until many other
things had taken place? Augustine suggests that the
angel spoke prophetically and that the words must be
taken in a symbolic sense. *Galilee* can be interpreted
either as *removal to another country* or as *revelation.*
Taken in the first sense, *Galilee* signifies the shift from
the people of Israel to the Gentiles, who would not
believe the apostles' preaching unless the Lord himself went before them on the way to prepare peoples'
hearts. When the angel says *"he goes before you into
Galilee; there you shall see him,"* he means, "You will
find the members of his Body, the church, in those
who welcome you."

When Galilee is understood to mean *revelation,*
the angel could mean that Christ will no longer be
seen in the form of a servant, but in that form in
which he is equal to the Father, as he promised those
who love him; so he goes before us to that place that
he had not left when he came to us, nor does he leave
us when he goes there ahead of us. That *revelation* will
be the true Galilee, when *we shall be like to him because
we shall see him as he is.*˙ And it will also be a more
blessed *emigration,* from this world to that eternity,

˙Cumm
Mark 16:7;
PL 30:641D

˙40 hom 21.4;
PL 76:1172A

˙Cumm
Mark 16:7;
PL 30:641D

˙1 John 3:2

provided we fulfill his commands in such a way as
to deserve to be set apart at his right hand.*

According to Gregory, since Galilee means *blessed
removal*, it is right to say that the Lord will be seen in
Galilee—whether because he has moved from corruption to incorruption and from mortality to immortality, or because those who have passed from
vice to virtue, from love of the world to love of God,
who have avoided evil and done good and have
sought for and known the things of heaven rather
than those of earth, will be found worthy to reach
the contemplation of his glory.[1]* About these words,
Jerome exclaims, "How few are the syllables *there
you shall see him*, but how vast are the promises they
contain! There is prepared the fountain of all our joys,
the source of our eternal salvation. There those who
were dispersed are gathered, there the contrite of
heart are healed. *There you shall see him*—but not as
you have seen him formerly."*

The women, however, were robbed of their hope
when they found the tomb empty. Giving no heed to
the angelic message they had heard, frightened out
of their wits by the extraordinary apparition of the
spirits, and weeping because they had not found the
Lord, they returned to the disciples and reported that
the Lord's body had been taken from the tomb. They
gave the disciples this news so that they would either
go and search with them or weep with them. They
said nothing about the angel or the announcement
that the Lord had risen—they simply told them that
the Lord was not in the tomb. *And these words seemed
to them as idle tales* and as something fantastic and

*De cons
ev 3.25; PL
34:1216

*40 hom 21.5;
PL 76:1172A

*Cumm
Mark 16:7;
PL 30:642A

---

[1] These interpretations of *Galilee* are based on Jerome, who gives
these Latin words for the Hebrew, meaning "circuit" or "round":
volutabilis (roll, think over), *transmigratio perpetrata* (removal accomplished), *rota* (rotate, wheel) (Int nom; PL 23:844).

untrue, that the Lord could have risen from the dead;

'Luke 24:11
and they did not believe them, because the idea that someone could rise from the dead was a novel one, and something completely unexpected. As Theophylact notes, "The miracle of resurrection is naturally

'En Ev Lc
24:1-12; PG
123:1111B
incredible to human beings."

Peter and John Run to the Tomb

Peter therefore went out, and the other disciple, that
'John 20:3
is, John; *and they came to the sepulcher.* Just as wood touched by fire bursts into flame without delay, so what they heard prompted them not to linger—their desire to know the facts impelled them to rush out. These two disciples loved Christ more than the others, and they almost considered one another brothers because they had spent so much time together, as we read in many places. *And they both ran together; and that other disciple,* being younger and more agile, *outran Peter and came first to the sepulcher, but he went not*
'John 20:4-5
in, out of respect for Peter; he waited for him, both because he was older and because he was the leader of the apostles. See how admirable they are! They run, and Mary Magdalen and her companions run after them: they all run, seeking their Lord heart and soul; they run faithfully, fervently, anxiously, eagerly. You, run after them—or better, keep up with them—and with them you will deserve to be comforted.

When they arrived at the tomb they peered in at the outer gate and then went in, first Peter and then John. John had arrived first, *but he went not in,* according to the literal meaning, out of respect for Peter, so he could enter first. But in a mystical sense, Gregory tells us, John represents the synagogue and Peter the church. The synagogue came to the tomb first but did not enter, because although it had known
'sacramenta
the mysteries* of Scripture first, yet it put off enter-

ing by embracing faith in the Lord's passion. The
church of the Gentiles followed behind *and went into
the sepulcher* because it knew Jesus Christ as dead in
the flesh and believed him to be the living God. But
John did go in after Peter, because at the end of the
world Judea will be brought to faith in the redeemer.*   *40 hom 22.3;
Going in, they did not find the body *but saw the*   PL 76:1175C
linen cloths in which his body had been wrapped
lying arranged and folded, *and the napkin that had
been about his head, not lying with the linen cloths, but
apart, wrapped up* neatly and carefully put *into one
place.** Everything had been done with such care that   *John 20:6-7
it was clear that the body had not been stolen and
that Christ's resurrection had taken place. But *they
saw and believed* what the women had said, that the
body of Christ had been taken from the tomb and
not that he had risen, for *as yet they knew not the Scripture** concerning Christ's resurrection, and the hidden   *John 20:9
meaning of it was not yet clear to them.
   They went away stunned with amazement and
marveled among themselves about what seemed to
have happened: how the linen cloths had been left
behind without the anointed corpse, and how in the
presence of armed guards a thief had had the op-
portunity to unravel the burial shrouds little by little
and carry the body off. It never occurred to them that
Christ had risen, nor did they realize that no one
would have carried off the body without also taking
the burial cloths, especially since the funeral ointment
would have made them cling to the corpse, and the
fact that they had been left behind—neatly folded—
made it very clear that he had risen. Chrysostom says,

> They saw the linen cloths lying, and the napkin
> that had been about his head, not lying with the
> linen cloths, but apart, wrapped up into one place,
> which was a sign of the resurrection. For if anyone
> had removed the body they would have taken

it as it was. If they had stolen it, they would not have stripped it first; nor would they have taken the trouble to remove the napkin, carefully fold it up, and set it in a place apart from the other cloths. This is also why John had mentioned the myrrh used in Jesus' burial, which would glue the linen to the body—so that you will not be fooled by those who claim that his body was stolen. Why do the burial clothes lie apart, with the napkin folded up by itself? So you may learn that this was not something done in haste, because the linen cloths were in one place and the napkin in another, and neatly folded at that. A grave robber would not be so foolish as to spend time on such an irrelevant task.*

*Hom John 85.4; PG 59:465

Gregory urges us to consider the greatness of the divine ordering of things: the disciples' hearts were moved to seek Jesus, but they were thwarted in finding him. In this way their weak minds, tormented by grief, would be purified in their desire to find him; the more difficult the search, the more intensely would they cling to the one they sought.* Feel compassion for the women and the disciples, for their grief was intense: they sought the Lord but could not find him—and they did not know where else to look.

*40 hom 22.5; PL 76:1177A

Angels Appear to the Women Again

Not wanting to linger by the tomb for fear of Jesus' enemies, the disciples, sorrowful and weeping, *departed again to their home,* that is, the hiding place from which they had ventured out in haste to the tomb; they still had no clear awareness of the Lord's resurrection. The three Marys stayed behind. *And they were astonished in their mind* at what they had seen: the women were amazed at seeing the large stone moved away, and sorrowful that Christ's venerable

*John 20:10

body was not there. Looking into the tomb, *they saw that two angels, looking like two men, stood by them in shining apparel,* in token of the joy of the Lord's resurrection. The angels proclaimed the Lord's victory not only by their words but also by their festive clothing. Angelic visitations take place for our instruction, and their appearance is consonant with their purpose: in this case, their brilliant vesture manifested the splendor of the occasion—they appeared *in shining apparel* to express the joy of the Lord's resurrection. Bede makes the following application: "Just as angels gathered to stand guard at the tomb containing the Lord's body, so we must believe that they assist at the eucharistic celebration when his most sacred Body is consecrated; as the apostle directs, women should cover their heads out of respect for the presence of angels in the church."

*Luke 24:4

*Com Luke 24:4; PL 92:623D

And as they were afraid because of this unexpected vision of angels, *they bowed down their faces toward the ground* out of reverence, and *the angels said to them,* to console them gently and instruct them about the resurrection of Christ, *"Why seek you the living* and already risen one *with the dead?"* This was as if to say, "Do not look for the one who has already risen from the dead here in this tomb, which is the abode of the dead." But how many *do* seek the living one among the dead! Even though they are good, they gladly keep company with the wicked. To such as these it could be said, *"Let the dead bury their dead."* And the angels went on, *"He is not here* in the tomb in his body, although in his presence as God he can never be absent, *but is risen* by his own power." And they added, to confirm what they were saying, *"Remember how he,* who is Truth and cannot lie, *spoke to you, when he was yet in Galilee, saying, 'The Son of man must be delivered into the hands of sinful men and be crucified and the third day rise again.'"* In other words, "He had

*Luke 24:5

*Matt 8:22

*Luke 24:6-7

predicted all these things long before they happened, so you should not be surprised that what you had heard has now come to pass." The women are told to remember his words, so that the proclamation of future events may be confirmed in faith by what has already been fulfilled.

The women were so awed by the appearance of the angels that they reverently lowered their faces to the ground. Bede writes, "Whenever we enter a church and draw near to the sacred mysteries, let us follow the example of these holy women's devotion to God: we should approach with humility and awe, whether because of the presence of the angelic powers or out of reverence for the holy sacrifice. Let us bow down to the ground before the countenance of the holy angels and, when we contemplate the eternal joy of the citizens of heaven, recall that we are but dust and ashes, as Abraham did: *I will speak to my Lord, whereas I am dust and ashes.*"*

*Gen 18:27; Com Luke 24:5; PL 92:624A

Those women paid no heed to the words of the angels; nor did they derive any comfort from seeing them—they were not seeking angels, but the Lord of angels. Two of them, Mary of James and Mary of Salome, were so frightened and distraught that, *going out, they fled from the sepulcher* and sat down some distance away. *A trembling and fear had seized them,* because of the angelic vision and the guards. *And they said nothing* to the angels who had spoken to them, or *to any man,** that is, to the guards, for they were afraid. As Augustine says, "We understand that they did not dare to say anything in response to the angels who had spoken to them, and certainly not to the guards whom they saw lying there."*

*Mark 16:8

*De cons ev 4.24.64; PL 34:1197

Lord Jesus Christ, only offspring of the Most High God, you instilled in the hearts of those who love you the desire to go in search of you, and you chose to deepen their desire by sending an angel to assure them

*that they would see you in Galilee. Grant that I, poor
as I am, may seek you ardently and rejoice to find you.
Moving from vice to virtue, and from love of this world
to love of you, by your grace may I deserve at the end of
this life to emigrate from time to eternity, so that with
all the elect I may see you, the God of gods in Sion,
that true Galilee. Amen.*

5

Christ Appears to Mary Magdalen

John 20:11-18

But Mary Magdalen, burning with love and brimming with bitterness, did not know what to do. She could not live without the teacher, but she did not find him here and had no idea where to look for him. In her fervor and constancy she *stood at the sepulcher* *without*, because the power of her emotion kept her
John 20:11 from sitting or lying down, *weeping** and lamenting her Lord. So deep was her love, so tender her devotion, and so strong the ties of charity that she scorned feminine frailty, and neither gloomy darkness nor the threat of the imminent arrival of her persecutors could drive her from her place beside the tomb. She remained behind when the other disciples departed, bathing the sepulcher in her tears. Such was the fire ignited by divine benevolence, so intense had her desire become, so deeply had she been wounded by love, that only tears gave her relief; she could truly say with the psalmist, *My tears have been my bread day*
Ps 41:4 *and night, while it is said to me daily: Where is your God?**

Augustine suggests that Mary's fervor and devotion were stronger than the other disciples' because her love was more passionate. She knew from experience what her tears could accomplish: she wept, and her sins were forgiven; she wept, and her brother was snatched out of the jaws of death; she wept, and she was consoled by the resurrection. Mary shed tears of
De cons ev contrition, compassion, and love.* Gregory says, "We
3.69, partial; must recall this woman's state of mind and the force
entire from
Albert, Com
John 20:11;
PL 34:1201

46

of the love that inflamed her. Even when the disciples had gone away, she did not leave the tomb. So it was that only the one who had stayed behind to seek him saw him. Perseverance is essential to good works."* And Augustine writes, "Although the men had returned home, a stronger affection kept the weaker sex rooted to the spot. The eyes that had sought for the Lord in vain now spoke in tears, expressing greater sadness at his absence from the tomb than for his death on the cross. The life of such a great teacher had been taken, and not even a memorial was left of him! Grief held this woman close to his grave."*

*40 hom 25.1; PL 76:1189C

*Tr John ev 121.1; PL 35:1995

Origen has a moving reflection on this scene:

> Brothers and sisters, we have heard that Mary was standing outside the tomb; we have heard that Mary wept. Love made her stay, sorrow made her weep. Her sadness was rekindled: where before she had mourned for him dead, now she mourned for him missing. This latter was more painful because there was no consolation to be had. She had wept for him in death, but at least she had the comfort of knowing that she could still see his body. This consolation was now snatched from her because his corpse was gone. The sight of him would have encouraged her devotion; she feared that the love for her master that burned in her heart would now grow cold.
>
> Mary wept more bitterly because her sorrow had been redoubled. In the depths of her being she bore a twofold burden, which she sought in vain to lessen with her tears. She remained where she was, weakening in body and soul, not knowing what to do next. Peter and John had been afraid, so they had fled. Mary felt no fear, because she could not imagine anything worse than what had already happened: she had lost the master whom she so singularly loved, and apart from him there was no object of her love or hope.

*Song 8:6

She had lost the life of her soul, so she thought it might be better to die than to live—perhaps in death she could find the one who eluded her in life. *Love is strong as death,* so what else was there for her to do?

She had become lifeless and numb. Feeling, she could not feel; seeing, she could not see; hearing, she could not hear. She could not be found where she was because she was with her Master—but she herself did not know where that was. She had looked for him but had not found him, and so she *stood at the sepulcher* and wept, tearful and sad. To be sure, Mary knew not what else to do, but to love and to shed tears for her beloved. She forgot her fear, indeed she forgot everything—everything but the one she loved above all others. All feeling had abandoned her, all thoughts, all hope. She could do only one thing: weep.[1]

*John 20:11

Now as she was weeping because Christ's body was gone, *she stooped down* bodily *and looked into the sepulcher,* because she continued to hope to find him where he had been buried; love fueled her search. When we lose something, we look for it everywhere, but we return frequently to the place where we remember last seeing it. So this woman looked here and there for the Lord's body, but in her anxiety she kept returning her gaze to the tomb where she knew he had been laid.

Gregory comments, "It is not enough for a lover to look once, because the force of love impels re-

---

[1] *Homilia de Maria Magdalena*, in Erasmus, *Origenis Adamantii Operum Pars Secunda* (Basel, 1545), 318–19. The *Homilia* is not by Origen but is a Latin work of the twelfth or thirteenth century. Although it is also attributed to Anselm or Gregory the Great, its true authorship is unknown. It is a very lively and dramatic work, and it circulated widely. Chaucer made an English translation of it (now lost) that he mentions in his *Legend of Good Women*: "He made also, gon is a gret while, Orygenes upon the Maudeleyne" (lines 427–28).

newed searching. She had looked before and not
found him; she persevered in seeking, and so it was
that she found him. Frustration increased her desires, and by increasing they found what they sought.
Holy desires are intensified by delay; if delay causes
them to die, they are not desires. Anyone capable
of straining after virtue has been inflamed by this
love."* One glance would not do: although Mary had
seen that Christ's body was gone, she went to the
tomb again to find out if there might be some trace of
it. She *stooped down* and peered into the tomb, giving
us to understand that we should ponder the death of
Christ with humility of heart; the fact that she *looked
in* again instructs us to ponder his death continually.

*40 hom
25.2; PL
76:1190A, C

The Angels in the Tomb

And with her bodily eyes *she saw the two angels in
white, sitting, one at the head, and one at the feet, where
the body of Jesus had been laid,*̇ out of reverence for the
place made holy by contact with the Lord's body. It
was Mary's intense devotion that merited this vision. *They said to her: "Woman, why do you weep?"*̇ By
forbidding tears, in a way the angels announce an
impending joy. It was as if they were saying, "Dry
your tears. You have cause for rejoicing, not weeping, because of Christ's resurrection. You should be
clapping, not crying; this is not a day for mourning,
but for joy. We have come to proclaim good news to
you, so do not weep; rather, look at him whom you so
greatly desire to see." Thinking that these were men,
not angels, and were ignorant of the situation, Mary
told them the reason for her tears: *"They have taken
away my Lord* from the tomb, *and I know not where
they have laid him.* Great sadness moves me to tears,
immense sorrow oppresses my heart."* She assumed
that either the guards or the Jewish leaders had made

*John 20:12

*John 20:13

*John 20:13

off with him and feared that they had dumped his
body in some disreputable place, resentful of the
honor paid it in this tomb, or had spirited it away
to desecrate it in some way. Such was her love that,
finding the tomb empty, she could only assume that
the body had been taken away. This caused her great
pain: since she did not know where it was, she could
not complete his burial rites.

See how marvelous is love's working! A little
earlier she had heard from one angel that Christ
was risen; now she hears from two of them that he
is alive. It does not sink in; all she can say is, *"I know
not."* Love acts like this because her soul is not with
her, but with her master. For, according to Origen,
Erasmus 322 Mary's soul was more in her teacher's body than in
her own. She cannot think, or speak, or hear about
anything but him: *"And I know not where they have laid
him."* This was the cause of her great sadness and
discouragement: she did not know where to go to
assuage her grief, because she did not know where
they had moved him. When Mary saw that the stone
had been rolled away, she believed that Christ had
been taken away. With the stone moved, it would
be easy to carry off the body, something that would
be impossible if the stone were in place. In the same
way, so long as the stone of the fear of God is in our
heart, Christ cannot be taken away from it, but if it
is removed, he can quickly be lost.

In What Way Christ Appeared to Mary Magdalen

The angels were powerless to comfort Mary as
she stood there crying. Her beloved, her teacher,
could keep himself from her no longer. The Lord
Jesus told his mother that he wished to go and console her. Bidding farewell, in a moment he was in the
garden with Mary Magdalen. As the woman stood

there weeping, Jesus, the comforter of the afflicted,
was present, contemplating her tears. He deigned to
appear behind her so that she would see him when
she turned away from the angels. This suggests that
you must turn to God if you want to see Jesus: those
who turn to God with all their heart will behold him.

Chrysostom asks, "Why did she not wait for the
angels to answer her question, but almost seemed
to ignore figures of such bearing when *she turned
round?*" I say it is because Christ came while Mary was   ˙John 20:14
speaking, and the angels stood out of reverence. See-
ing this, Mary turned around to see what had made
them stand up."* *And she knew not that it was Jesus,*†   ˙Hom John
because she did not see him in his glorified state,   86.1; PG
as the angels did who paid him homage. Because   59:468
she did not yet believe in the resurrection, Christ ap-   †John 20:14
peared to her in the kind of body that she pictured
in her mind. Bernard exclaims, "O, what a touching
expression of devotion! He who is desired and sought
both hides himself and reveals himself. He hides so
that he might be sought the more ardently; having
been longed for, he will be found with greater joy;
having been found he will be held more tenaciously;
being held more tenaciously, he will not be lost."*   ˙Drogo,
According to Gregory, "Mary still doubted the Lord's   Sermo de
resurrection: even though she turned around to see   pass; PL
Jesus, by doubting she turned her back on the Lord's   166:1539C
face, whom she did not believe had risen. Because
she both loved and doubted, she saw him but did
not recognize him: love revealed him to her, doubt
concealed him."*   ˙40 Hom
                                                              25.4; PL
Jesus said to her: "Woman, why are you weeping?   76:1192B
Whom do you seek?" † Gregory says that Jesus asks the
reason for her sorrow to increase her desire, so that   †John 20:15
when he asked whom she was seeking she would
feel greater love for him.* Not knowing who he was,   ˙40 hom 25.4;
Mary assumed that he was the gardener responsible   PL 76:1192B

for the grounds where the tomb was located. Because
he was there so early in the morning, she concluded
that only the gardener would have business there at
that hour. And, in a spiritual sense, he really *was* a
gardener to her, because he had already pulled the
weeds of infidelity and evil from her heart, and, having cleared the ground, he had planted the good seed
of faith and virtue in her with his love and power.

The job of a gardener is to get rid of weeds and
make good plants grow. And each day the Lord
weeds his garden, the church, so that the plants of
virtue can flourish. Origen asks,

> O Mary, if you are seeking Jesus, why do you not
> recognize him? Look, the Jesus for whom you
> are searching comes to you, and you think he is
> the gardener. He is what you take him to be, but
> you are also mistaken: while you recognize him
> to be the gardener, you do not recognize him to
> be Jesus. For he is Jesus and he is the gardener:
> he sows every good seed in the garden of your
> soul and in the hearts of his faithful. He himself
> plants and waters every good gift in the hearts
> of his saints, and it is this Jesus with whom you
> are speaking.*

*Erasmus 322

He appeared in the guise of a gardener to Mary Magdalen because this office, this work, this exercise, and
this title are suitable for beginners: penitents must
work as gardeners, pulling the weeds of vice and
planting the seeds of virtue. If you want him to act as
your gardener, you must uproot the noxious plants
and replace them with wholesome ones.

But she, distraught, spoke to him as the gardener,
saying, *"Sir, if you have taken him from here, tell me
where you have laid him,* for even in death he is my one
treasure, *and I will* receive him with all devotion and

*John 20:15

take him away."* She addressed the gardener as *Sir* to
win his favor, and she did not say "if you have taken

away the crucified Jesus," giving a precise description or name, but simply said *him*. Such is the power of love and the devotion of the seeker, so fervently is such a one accustomed to think of the beloved that she assumes that everyone else must know who she is thinking of and searching for and cannot imagine that anyone would be ignorant of his identity. *"If you have taken him from here* for fear of his enemies, *tell me where* and *I will take him away."* She feared that Jesus' enemies would inflict more humiliation on him in death, and she wanted to take his body away to a hidden location.

What remarkable courage this woman shows, who does not shy away from seeing a dead body and asserts that she can move a heavy corpse unaided! The force of her devotion convinced her that she could carry his heavy body alone, because a person in love sees no insuperable difficulties. Other women might think they could not sustain the weight of a dead body, or would be afraid to handle a corpse; Mary's love led her to believe that the task would be both possible and easy. Origen says, "Joseph was afraid and did not dare to remove Christ's body from the cross without Pilate's permission, and then only under cover of darkness. But Mary did not wait for nightfall or ask permission or cringe before anyone; she boldly promised, *'I will take him away.'* O wondrous audacity of this woman! Woman no longer a 'mere woman'! She gives no ground, she does not quibble; she speaks fearlessly and promises absolutely, *'Tell me where you have laid him, and I will take him away.'* O Mary, how great are your constancy and your faith!"* Mary Magdalen showed here her great devotion and fervent love, and so she deserved to see and hear alive the one she sought dead. Study her well, how her tearstained face humbly and devoutly persuades the stranger to show her where to find the one she sought, how she

*Erasmus
322–23

continually hopes to learn something new about the person she cherished above all others.

*John 20:16

*Jesus said to her: "Mary."** As Gregory points out, when Jesus addressed her as *woman,* the common name for all of her sex, she had not recognized him. Now he calls her by her proper name so that she will look at him more intently and, by realizing who he really is, put an end to the affliction caused by her desire. He says to her, *"Mary,"* showing that he knows who she is. It is as if he were saying, "Recognize him

*40 hom 25.5; PL 76:1192D

who recognizes you."** God certainly knows the full number of the elect, but he gives a particular blessing to some of them when, by using their proper names, he makes it clear that they are known by God.

She turned with her heart and the eyes of her soul, where before she had turned only with her body and physical eyes; as soon as she heard her name spoken, she recognized the voice of the Good Shepherd. When she turned with her body, she thought Jesus to be what he was not; now that she had turned with her heart, she knew him. Like one brought back to life, she adored him with ineffable joy, and *said to him: "Rabboni!" (which is to say, Master).** You are the one I

*John 20:16

have been seeking—why have you hidden yourself so long from me? So she persevered in order to seek, and she strained in order to find. Gregory says, "Because Mary was called by name, she recognized her creator, and called him at once *Rabboni,* that is, 'Teacher.' He was both the one she was outwardly seeking and the one who was instructing her inwardly to seek

*40 hom 25.5; PL 76:1193A
*Ps 76:11

him."** And Origen exclaims, "O, *this is the change of the right hand of the Most High*!* Indescribable sorrow is turned to ineffable joy, tears of mourning into tears of love and elation! As soon as she heard this word, *Mary,* by which her teacher addressed her, she had a presentiment in the sweet speaking of her name

*Erasmus 323

that the one who so addressed her was her Lord."**

And Anselm writes,

Do not abandon Magdalen's company, but, having prepared the spices with her, make sure you visit the Lord's tomb. O, that you may see in spirit what she saw with her own eyes: now, the angel sitting on the stone rolled away from the tomb; now, inside the tomb, one angel at the head and the other at the foot, proclaiming the glory of the resurrection; now, Christ the Lord gazing with loving eyes on Mary, sorrowful and weeping, and saying to her, *"Mary."* The floodgates are opened at the sound of this word, tears are drawn from the core of her being, sobs and sighs well up from the depths of her heart. O blessed Mary, what stirred in your mind and heart when, on hearing this voice, you prostrated yourself and answered back, *"Rabboni"*? I ask, with what affection, with what emotion, did you cry out, *"Rabboni"*? Tears now prevent further talk: emotions silence all speech, and a wave of love overwhelms the senses of soul and body.˙

˙Aelred,
De inst 31
[Anselm
Med 15]; PL
158:792A

And elsewhere,

The Lord speaks the customary name of his handmaid, and the handmaid recognizes the well-known voice of the Lord. I believe, indeed I assert, that she recognized the familiar sweetness with which he pronounced her name. O charming voice, O with what gentleness and love you pronounce it! It cannot be said more briefly: "I know who you are, I know what you seek." Immediately, tears are transformed. I do not think they ceased, but where formerly they were squeezed from a contrite heart, now they flow from a heart full of joy. How different are the two exclamations: *"Rabboni!"* and, *"If you have taken him from here, tell me where!"* or *"They have taken away my Lord, and I know not where they have laid him,"* and *"I have seen the Lord; and these things he said to me."*˙

˙Anselm, 74;
=Oratio
74 [16];
PL 158:1012A

Running forward and falling before Jesus, Mary immediately wanted to adore his very footprints, and to hold and kiss his feet, as was her custom. O strong and eager love! It was not enough to see Jesus and speak with him, she also had to touch him; she knew that *virtue went out from him and healed all.* He, however, wanting to play the part of a gardener by planting the seed of faith in her heart and to raise her soul to heavenly things, said to her, *"Do not touch me* with your bodily hands, because you have not yet touched me by the faith in your heart."* It was as if he were saying, "I would prefer that you touch me with the touch of your soul, believing me to be equal to the Father, than that you touch me physically, believing me to be only human, and so less than the Father." To this point she had wept for him as man because she only believed in him in an earthly way. She was forestalled because her faith was deficient, and this was why she was not worthy to touch him.

And so Jesus added, *"for I am not yet ascended* in your heart *to my Father,* as being his equal. You do not believe that as the Son I am equal to and coeternal with the Father, who raised me from the dead; you came to carry off one who was only a corpse." In other words, "Because you come looking for me in the tomb as one dead and do not believe I have risen, you do not deserve to touch me who am alive. You seek the living among the dead, and so for you *I am not yet ascended to my Father*; when I ascend to the Father in your understanding, then you will deserve to touch me as the Father's equal." Anselm asks,

*Luke 6:19

*John 20:17

*John 20:17

> But why, good Jesus, prevent the one who loves you from touching your holy and most desired feet? Why do you say, *"Do not touch me"*? Why may I not touch those pierced feet from which your blood flowed for my sake? Why may I not hold them and kiss them? Are you more unrecep-

tive than usual because you are more glorious? Look, I am not going to withdraw from you or abandon you. If I cannot touch you, my tears will not cease, my heart will burst from its sighing. And he answers, "Do not be afraid: I am not taking away this blessing, I am keeping it for later."*

*Aelred, De inst 31 [Anselm Med 15]; PL 158:792B

Thus Mary had to prepare herself by struggling with doubts and disquieting grief before she would be permitted to touch such holiness. If she, who was privileged to be the first to see the risen Christ after his mother, and who was so loved by the one who had delivered her from all of her sins, was prevented from touching his feet, how much more should those who are polluted by sin refrain from touching him by celebrating Mass or receiving Holy Communion?

Mary Magdalen, the Apostle to the Apostles

Then Jesus said, "But *go* joyfully *to my brethren* the apostles *and say to them*: 'Now that I have risen from the dead, I will *ascend to my Father* (by generation and nature) *and to your Father* (by adoption and grace), *to my God* (because he created me as man, and in my human nature I am less than he) *and to your God** (because he created you, freed you from error, and made me the mediator between you and him).'" In other words, he was telling them that soon they would see him ascend. He spoke these words insofar as he was human; *ascending* does not pertain to his divine nature, which is always most high. This is made clear by the fact that he calls the apostles *brethren*, on account of his conformity with human nature, the spiritual bond of friendship, and the grace of adoption; they are the Father's sons by adoption, but he is the Son by nature. Severian says, "He calls them brothers who have truly become his brothers by virtue of his taking on human nature; he calls them brothers

*John 20:17

whom his Father has adopted as sons; he calls them brothers whom the kind Jesus has made his coheirs; he calls them brothers because of the special bond of friendship that unites them." * And Ambrose: "You descended as the Son of Man, but you did not leave the Father in descending. You descended to us so that we could see you with our eyes and with our minds and so believe in you. Ascend now from us, so that we can follow you with our minds although we cannot see you with our eyes." *

*Chrysologus, Sermo 80; PL 52:427A

*Exp ev Luke 10.159; PL 15:1843D

These two stand together talking to one another with great joy and pleasure, as friend speaks to friend. Behold, here is the great Easter feast! Upon leaving his mother, the Lord *appeared first to Mary Magdalen* before anyone else, even the apostles themselves. Jerome observes, "He showed himself first to Mary Magdalen, *out of whom he had cast seven devils*, because *the publicans and the harlots shall go into the kingdom of God before* the synagogue, just as the thief entered in before the apostles." *

*Mark 16:9

*Matt 21:31

*Cumm Mark 16:9; PL 30:642B

Let us imitate this woman: she arose very early, wept very bitterly, loved very ardently, sought very diligently, and so found before anyone else. Let us seek the Lord by carrying out our religious duties with tears and perseverance; with Mary we will find the Lord and deserve to be consoled by him. Origen urges us,

> Dear brothers and sisters, let us imitate this holy woman's disposition so that we can reach her position. Let each of us weep for Jesus, and earnestly seek Jesus, for he is never absent. *The Lord is good to the soul that seeks him.* * Learn, O sinful man, from the sinful woman, whose sins were all forgiven her; learn, sinner, to weep for the God who is absent, and long with all your heart for him to be present. Learn from Mary to love Jesus, to hope in Jesus, and constantly to seek Jesus, and

*Lam 3:25

by your seeking track him down. Let no obstacle prevent you; accept no consolation apart from Jesus; despise everything apart from him. Learn from Mary to search for Jesus in the sepulcher of your heart; move the stone from the entrance to God's tomb; banish all hardness and repel every obstacle to your faith. Remove all concupiscence and impurity from your heart, and search high and low carefully to see if Jesus is there.

If you do not find Jesus within yourself, stand outside and weep; stand resolute in faith, look carefully at others who are outside, on the chance that you may find him and see him in them; with tears beg Jesus to enter into you and remain with you. And, lest your stiff-necked pride drive him away, humbly bow your head and look again into the tomb of God, which should be within you: there you might catch sight of two angels, one at the head and the other at the foot. That is, you may perceive within yourself heavenly desires, whether for the contemplative life or the active; but even with these, if you are not able to see or possess Jesus, do not settle for this, do not be content with this deficiency: weep and go in search of Jesus himself within you until you find him.

And if by chance he should appear to you in some other form and according to your desire manifest himself to you, do not presume that it is because of your merit or desire that he appears to you. Rather, attribute this gift to his goodness and benevolence: question him and pray to him to reveal himself to you. I dare to promise you with confidence that if you stand in faith at the tomb of your heart, if you go in search of Jesus with tears and persevere in your searching, if you bow down in humility, if like Mary you accept no consolation but Jesus himself and only in the way he chooses to reveal himself, without doubt you will find him, and you will know him. You will not need to ask others where Jesus is—you will

*John 20:18;
Erasmus 323

be able to point him out to others, proclaiming, *"I have seen the Lord, and these things he said to me."* *

The Lord departed after a brief delay, explaining that he needed to visit others. Having received a blessing from the Lord before his departure, Mary Magdalen also left. Believing now in the resurrection, she found her companions and told them what had happened. The news of Christ's resurrection gave the women great joy, although they were sorry they had not seen him. *And they went out quickly from* the place in front of *the sepulcher with fear and great joy, running*

*Matt 28:8

to tell his disciples * about these things. We read in the Gloss that two emotions struggled within them: fear, because of the magnitude of the miracle, and joy, because of their desire to see the risen Christ. These

*Jerome,
Com Matt
28:8; PL
26:217A;
Gloss: PL
114:177C

contending emotions gave wings to their feet. *

> *O most loving Lord, most gracious Master, how good you are to those who are right of heart, how gentle with those who love you! They are fortunate who seek you, and blessed whose hope you are! Truly, you love all those who love you and never abandon those who hope in you. This loving woman sincerely sought you and truly found you. She hoped in you, and you did not abandon her: indeed, she obtained from you far more than she hoped for. Lord, give me the grace to love you, seek you, and hope in you; may I deserve to be loved by you, and, having found you, never be forsaken by you. Amen.*

6

Christer Appears to the Three Marys

Matt 28:9-10; John 20:18

As the three Marys were making their way back to
the apostles in the city, *behold*, the Lord *Jesus* appeared
and *met them.* Jerome says, "They were going to the   ˙Matt 28:9
apostles so that through them the seedbed of faith
would be planted."* They were worthy to encounter   ˙Com Matt
the risen Lord on the way because they sought dili-   28:9; PL
gently and hurried with such purpose. This shows,   26:217A
according to Rabanus Maurus, that Christ comes to
our aid as soon as we begin to walk in the path of
virtue and helps us attain eternal salvation.* By a   ˙Hom 21; PL
pleasant word of greeting—*Ave*, reversing *Eva*—he   110:184A
lifted their spirits and consoled them in their sorrow.
Jerome observes, "The women deserved to be the
first to hear *Ave*, so that the woman Eve's curse was
undone among women."*   ˙Com Matt
    But they, filled with a joy beyond description, *came*   28:9; PL
up and took hold of his feet, devoutly kissing them with   26:217A
the clear recognition that his human body had been
raised from the dead, *and adored him.* In approach-   ˙Matt 28:9
ing Christ they showed that they were believers enlightened by faith, for as the apostle teaches, *"He that*
comes to God must believe." Chrysostom writes,   ˙Heb 11:6

> Running to him with great joy, *they took hold of his*
> *feet* and received by touch incontrovertible proof
> of his resurrection, *and they adored him*. Perhaps
> you would like to imitate these women and cling
> to Jesus' feet. You can do that now: and not only
> his feet and hands—you can even hold his sacred

head and receive the awesome mysteries with a pure conscience. But not only now; if you show mercy, you will also see him when he comes in ineffable glory, escorted by the angelic hosts, and you will hear him say, *"Come, you blessed of my Father, possess you the kingdom prepared for you from the foundation of the world."**

*Matt 25:34;
Hom Matt
89.3; PG
57/58:781

We receive forgiveness by drawing near to Christ's feet. Let us throw ourselves at those feet and kiss them by our devout prayer, contemplating his humanity. If you want to lay hold of the majesty of God, first take hold of Christ's humanity. In a moral sense, we approach Christ through the light of faith, as it says in the Psalms: *Come to him and be enlightened;** we cling to him through unitive love, as we read in the Song of Songs: *"I held him* (the beloved) *and I will not let him go";** and we adore him by worshiping him, as this gospel teaches: *You shall adore the Lord your God, and him only shall you serve.**

*Ps 33:6

*Song 3:4

*Matt 4:10

Mary Magdalen was now allowed to touch him. This had been denied her earlier, when she was seeking the living one among the dead, that is, in the burial place of the sepulcher. They all spoke to one another with great rejoicing, celebrating a solemn Pasch. Anselm urges us, "Stay here as long as you can. Do not let sleep interrupt your delights or external distractions disrupt them."*

*Aelred,
De inst 31
[Anselm
Med 15]; PL
158:792C

Then Jesus said to them: "Fear not." He said this to give them peace of mind, because the dread that had overwhelmed them had not yet left them completely. Just as Jesus had met them as they were hurrying away and given them joy by his greeting, so now he banished their fears. And he added, *"Go, tell my brethren to go into Galilee. There they shall see me."** Jerome comments, "Not into Judea, but into a place among the Gentiles, to show that grace will move from Judea

*Matt 28:10

to the nations, and that he is going ahead to prepare the hearts of the Gentiles."*

Here again we see the teacher of humility calling his disciples brothers, speaking of them in more affectionate terms than usual. He did this so that they would not hesitate to draw near to him, held back by fear because they had deserted him when he was arrested, so that he could teach them the truth of his resurrection, and so that he could enkindle their love and devotion. In order to give due honor to the Lord, the angel had been moved for the sake of humility to call them *disciples*; Jesus himself, although he is the Lord, was motivated by both charity and humility to call them *brothers*.

Jesus, the Lord of all, never ceased being humble: he was faithful to this virtue unto death, and after death, and even after his ascension. Did he not wash his disciples' feet on the last night of his life? Did he not show humility beyond description by mounting the infamous gibbet of the cross? After his resurrection, did he not call his disciples *brothers*? After his ascension, did he not speak humbly to Saul, almost as to an equal, when he said, *"Saul, Saul, why do you persecute me?"* * Nor, on that occasion, did he speak of himself as God, but as *Jesus of Nazareth*. And when he is enthroned in glory to judge the world, will he not speak those soothing words, *"As long as you did it to one of these my least brethren, you did it to me"*? * It was with good reason that he loved this virtue so much and commended it to us so highly by his example, for without humility as a foundation it is impossible to build a home with the other virtues. Do not rely on chastity, or poverty, or any other virtue or good work, if humility is absent.

*Rabanus Maurus, Matt 28:10; PL 107:1149D; partial Jerome, Com Matt 28:10 [PL 26:217C]

*Acts 9:4

*Matt 25:40

Apostles to the Apostles

Then *Mary Magdalen* and the other two women *came* to announce the good news of Christ *and told the disciples*, who were mourning Christ's death, *"I have seen the Lord, and these things he said to me,** and commissioned me to report them to you."* These women were truly evangelists, acting as apostles to the apostles, hastening *to show forth your mercy in the morning.** Each person who understands rightly should proclaim the truth to others, as it says in the book of Revelation: *"He that hears, let him say: 'Come.'"** Therefore, this woman, the first to see the risen Lord because she was more eager than all the others to see Christ's tomb, symbolizes anyone who ardently seeks knowledge of divine truth and for this reason deserves to attain it. Such a one is obliged to share this truth with others, just as Magdalen announced it to the disciples, so as not to be condemned for concealing her talent. Bede says, "By announcing to the disciples that Christ had risen, this woman reminds all of us, and especially those who exercise the office of preaching, that whenever we receive a revelation of heavenly truth we should eagerly share it with our neighbors."*

This incident manifests God's abundant mercy to the female sex. It is to a woman that the mystery of the resurrection was first proclaimed; it was first entrusted to her watchful care, so that the old transgression might be abolished. As Gregory says, "The sin of the human race was uprooted where it began: in Paradise, the woman handed death to the man; from the sepulcher the woman proclaimed life to the men. She who had related the words of the death-dealing serpent now announced the words of the one who had brought her to life. It was as if the Lord was telling the human race, not by word but by action, 'Receive the elixir of life from the same

*John 20:18

*Ps 91:3

*Rev 22:17

*CA John 20:10-18, citing Bede

hand that gave you the potion of death.'"* Woman, who had been the gateway to death, was the first to proclaim the resurrection and by doing so pointed out the door of life. Augustine says, "The women first announced Christ's rising to the apostles. Woman had announced death to her man in Paradise; women announced salvation to the men in the church. The apostles were to proclaim the resurrection of Christ to the nations—but it was the women who proclaimed it to the apostles."*

*40 hom 25.6; PL 76:1194B

And Ambrose writes, "Just as at the beginning the woman was the author of the man's transgression, and man the executor of the error, so now the first to have tasted death is the first to behold the resurrection. She leads the way in both the offense and the remedy. And, so that the weight of her guilt would not continue to weigh people down, she who had served up the Fall also decanted the grace; by proclaiming the resurrection she compensated for her original transgression. Death had issued from a woman's mouth, and life is restored through a woman's mouth."*

*Sermo 51.2.3; PL 38:335

And, finally, let us listen to Bede: "How fortunate were these women, who were found worthy to proclaim the triumph of the resurrection to the world and to announce that death's realm, to which Eve became subject when beguiled by the serpent's speech, had been shattered! How much more fortunate will be the souls of all those—men and women alike—who, helped by heavenly grace to triumph over death, will be found worthy to enter into the joy of a blessed resurrection, while the reprobate are struck with fear and justly punished on the Day of Judgment!"*

*Com Luke 10.156; PL 15:1834B

We see how fitting it is that this woman should be the first to proclaim the joy of the Lord's resurrection when we recall that seven demons had been

*Hom ev 2.1 [2.7]; PL 94:136D

*Rom 5:20

cast out of her, that is, every kind of sin and vice. This shows that where sin abounded, grace abounded all the more.* The fact that someone who had been the slave of so many vices was raised immediately to such eminence that she evangelized the very evangelists and apostles themselves with the miracle of the resurrection assures all who are truly repentant that they should never despair that their sins can be forgiven. This also reminds us that none of us should presume on our own innocence and disparage others as sinners—sometimes by God's grace when a sinner gets up after falling, his condition is better than it was before he fell. When good people sin, the stone is moved, but it is not rejected. The just fall, the just slip; but when the just get up again, they are better. Truly, with the saints *all things work together unto good.**

*Rom 8:28

> O Jesus, our ransom, our love, and our desire, at your resurrection you graciously chose to appear to the devout women who were longing for you and seeking you as they returned from your tomb. Dearest Jesus, I too seek you, whom my soul loves; I seek, but I do not find. Come to meet me as I search for you, O only-begotten Son of the Father, and even if you withhold your longed-for presence now, do not do so in the future. In the final resurrection of your faithful, show yourself to be kind and gentle with me as you are with them, so that with the elect I may be found worthy to rejoice in your presence forever. Amen.

7

Christ Appears to Peter,
Joseph of Arimathea,
James the Less,
and the Holy Ancestors

When Mary Magdalen and her companions returned home and told the disciples that Christ had
risen, Peter was sad because he had not seen his Lord.
Such was his love that he could not sit there quietly
but left the others to look for the Lord, going by himself to the sepulcher. He did not know where else to
look. While he was still on the way *the Lord appeared
to Simon,* although the evangelist does not say where   ˙Luke 24:34
and when this took place. When Peter saw the Lord,
he prostrated himself on the ground and begged
forgiveness for his desertion and denials; the Lord
forgave him his sins, gently consoled him, and instructed him to confirm his brethren. They then stood
conversing joyfully with one another for a while and
so celebrated a great Pasch. Christ appeared to Peter
alone, because Peter alone had denied him.

Among the people mentioned by the evangelists
and apostles, the Lord desired to appear first to Peter
for many reasons. First, he had been the first to confess him to be the Christ, so he deserved to be the first
to see him alive again. Second, to restore his peace
of mind, which had been shattered by the passion;
since his fear had led him to the most dramatic fall,
he should be the first to rise again through the hope
given by the resurrection. Third, to show him that he
had been forgiven for his threefold denial, comforting

him lest he despair. Fourth, to restore the apostle to his position among the Twelve and strengthen him in it. Fifth, to show him in action how to deal mercifully with sinners under his authority, no matter how great their offense. Sixth, to give hope for mercy and forgiveness to all sinners by showing that Christ did not view them with contempt.

A seventh reason is suggested by John Chrysostom: "He did not show himself to everyone at the same time so that he might sow the seeds of faith. He who saw him first, and was thereby convinced, was to carry the news to the others; the word going forth would prepare the souls of its hearers to see Christ. Tremendous faith was required of the one who first saw the risen Christ, so that he would not be confounded by such an unexpected sight. But the Lord appeared to others after Peter, at one time to fewer, at another time to more."* Having received a blessing from Christ, Peter returned to our Lady and the disciples and told them everything; from then on he remained very faithful to God in all things. *Peter* is interpreted as *obedient*; by his example he shows that the Lord is accustomed to appear frequently to those who practice obedience.

*Hom
1 Cor 38.4;
PG 61:327

Joseph of Arimathea

Taking leave of Peter, Jesus next appeared to Joseph of Arimathea, who had given Jesus burial in his own tomb. We read in the *Gospel of the Nazarenes* that the Jewish leaders were irate when they heard that Joseph had asked Pilate for Jesus' body and had given it honorable burial in his own sepulcher. On the very night of Christ's burial they seized Joseph and locked him securely in a small room. They bound him to a column in this prison, intending to kill him after the Sabbath. But behold! On the very day of resurrection four angels lifted this house into the air, and Jesus went in and joyfully appeared to Joseph. He comforted him, wiped the tears from his face, and kissed him; then, with the seals still in place on the doors, he freed Joseph from the confines of his room and brought him to his home in Arimathea.[1]

See how the Lord does not forget his own or abandon them but at length consoles and helps them at the proper time, for he is *a refuge for the poor, a helper in due time in tribulation.** As Chrysostom says, "This is most certainly the way God acts: when evil deeds are heaped upon his people, and he sees them gravely afflicted and their enemies carried away by cruelty toward them, then God manifests his own power by signs."* As to Nicodemus, who helped his companion Joseph bury his Lord, they say that during this time he went into hiding for fear of the Jewish leaders. *Joseph* is interpreted as *increase*, or *length of days*, and he stands for those who persevere in good works, to whom the Lord himself frequently deigns to appear.

James the Less

The Lord appeared that same day to James the Less, as is mentioned in the First Letter to the Corinthians.* At the Last Supper this apostle had vowed that he would not touch any food after he drank from the Lord's chalice until he saw him risen from the dead. So when James had still not tasted any food by the day of the resurrection, the Lord appeared to him and those who were with him and said, "Set your table and put out the bread." Then he took the bread, blessed it, broke it, and gave it to James, saying, "My brother, eat your bread, because the Son of Man has

---

[1] The story is related in the *Acts of Pilate* 15.6, which is appended to the apocryphal *Gospel of Nicodemus*. See J. K. Elliott, *Apocryphal New Testament* (New York: Oxford University Press, 1993), 182.

*De vir ill 2; PL 23:613A

risen from the dead." Josephus tells this story, as does Jerome in his book *De viris illustribus*.*[2]

Note that James was hungering not only for substantial bread but also for supersubstantial bread, that is, for Jesus himself, and so he deserved to be filled with both the one and the other. The Lord does not permit those who hunger for him or go hungry for his sake to faint away from starvation—rather, he gives those who hope in him food in due season and fills them with blessings. James* is interpreted as *wrestler*, and he provides an example for those who show courage in their struggle with temptation and zeal in uprooting their faults; to such as these the Lord also shows himself often. So, reader, strive to be Peter by obeying, James by overcoming temptations, and Joseph by progressing from virtue to virtue; then the Lord will not neglect to visit you through his grace and give you the consolation that he knows you need.

*Jacob

It must be obvious that the soul to whom the Lord deigns to show himself in any form whatever is never left without consolation and some kind of beneficial revelation; all the resurrection appearances make this quite clear. He appeared promptly and gloriously to his mother Mary, who had experienced the harshest grief at his death and who consequently awaited his resurrection with the greatest eagerness; so completely was her sorrow turned to joy that all her former pains were forgotten. Similarly, when he appeared to Mary Magdalen in the guise of a gardener, he comforted her in the midst of her tears simply by speaking her name, *"Mary."* At this word she immediately turned around, and, consoled by the

---

[2] Jerome quotes the *Gospel of the Hebrews*, an early Jewish Christian gospel that survives only in a few patristic references. Josephus does not describe this incident but does mention the martyrdom of "James, the brother of Jesus" in AD 62 (*Antiquities* 20.9.1).

knowledge that it was the Lord, she exclaimed with great joy, *"Rabboni!"* Then the Lord revealed to her the mystery of his will, saying, *"Go to my brothers and tell them I am ascending to my Father."* *

    Likewise, when he encountered the three women on the way, he gave them great solace by saying, *"Ave,"* and adding, *"Do not be afraid."* Then he revealed his mystery to them, saying, *"Go, tell my brothers that they are to go to Galilee, and there they will see me."* * And in the same way, when he appeared to the two disciples on the road in the form of a fellow traveler, he opened up for them the meaning of the Scriptures and made their hearts burn and finally consoled them by revealing himself fully to them in the breaking of the bread. He also brought great comfort to his disciples when they were gathered in one place and he appeared to them in his own form, saying: *"Peace be with you. Why are you disturbed? It is I, do not be afraid. See my hands and my feet."* And he opened their minds that they might understand the Scriptures. *

    And so with all the resurrection appearances: in whatever form he took, God consoled those who saw him with some kind of revelation; nor should it be doubted that he will always give consolation to those he loves. Be mindful that divine consolation can be acquired in several ways: first, by holy fear; second, by tears of devotion; third, by bearing with tribulation; fourth, by humbling oneself; fifth, by shunning worldly consolations; and sixth, by contemplating heavenly realities.

*John
20:16-17

*Matt 28:9-10

*Luke
24:36-45

The Holy Ancestors

    Then the Lord withdrew because he had not yet visited with the holy ancestors since his resurrection; he had left them in the Paradise of delights. He returned to them, clothed in brilliant vesture and accompanied by a multitude of angels. Seeing him in such glory from a long way off, they welcomed him with indescribable joy and exultation, singing hymns and canticles and prostrating themselves before him in adoration. Then, getting to their feet and standing before him, they fervently concluded their praises with all the devotion in their power. O, how many and how profound were the joys there, where the whole assembly of saints sang as one! O, how good and pleasant it is to be in the midst of this throng, or even to perceive it from a distance! Draw near to them yourself, and, if you are permitted, join your praises to theirs, or at least listen to them from a distance and take delight in them.

> *Lord Jesus Christ, grant that I may be a Peter by obeying, a James by overcoming faults, and a Joseph by advancing from virtue to virtue. As I persevere patiently in this path, deign to visit me often with your grace, as you deigned to appear to your disciples in their distress. May I share in the joy that those holy ancestors felt who were found worthy to see you in glory after your resurrection, and may I too be found worthy to rejoice forever with them in your presence, with that same ineffable joy they know now in heaven with you. Amen.*

8

The Lord Appears to Two Disciples on the Road to Emmaus

Luke 24:13-35

And behold, on that same day of the Lord's resurrection *two of the* seventy-two *disciples* of Christ *went to a town which was sixty furlongs* to the west *from Jerusalem, named Emmaus. And they,* driven almost to despair because of Jesus' fate, *talked together of all these things which had happened*—especially about his life and death, and how they knew that he had been put to death even though he was completely innocent. *And it came to pass that while they talked and reasoned with themselves* in their grief, *Jesus himself also, drawing near, went with them.* He walked with them as a fellow traveler, asking them questions and responding to their own, speaking beneficial words to them so that, in Bede's opinion, he could kindle in their hearts the flame of faith in his resurrection and also fulfill in reality what he had once promised: *"Where there are two or three gathered together in my name, there am I in the midst of them."**

*Luke 24:13-15

*Matt 18:20; Com Luke 24:15; PL 92:625D

Because they loved the Lord in their hearts but doubted his resurrection, the Lord appeared to them in bodily form, but they did not know who he was. What they beheld outwardly with their eyes reflected what was happening inwardly in their hearts. They saw, because they loved—but, because they doubted, they did not know whom they were seeing. And so the sacred text says, *But their eyes were held, that they should not know him.* Their incredulity and doubt

*Luke 24:16

73

prevented them from recognizing Christ in bodily form. Their eyes perceived what was true, not what was false; however, it was not Jesus but their own incredulity that kept them from seeing the whole truth. According to Augustine, "If Mark tells us that the Lord appeared to them *in another form*, here Luke refers to the same thing by saying *their eyes were held, that they should not know him.* Something had come upon their eyes that was to remain there until the breaking of the bread. The Lord certainly could have transformed his body so that his form and figure would have been different from what they were ac-customed to, but he in fact did not do this."[*]

*De cons ev 25.72; PL 34:1206

And he said to them: "What are these conversations that you hold one with another as you walk and are sad?"[*] They were conversing between themselves as if they no longer expected to see Christ alive and were sor-rowful because the Savior was dead. *And the one of them, whose name was Cleophas, answering, said to him: "Are you only a stranger in Jerusalem, and do not know the things that have been done there in these days?"*[*] The-ophylact comments, "It is as if he said, 'You alone seem to be some kind of stranger living outside the confines of Jerusalem, so that you are unaware of what has taken place there.'"[*] And Bede: "They thought he was a stranger because they did not rec-ognize his face. But in truth he was a stranger to them because he was so far removed from the fragility of their natures by virtue of the glory of his resurrection. Because they were not informed of his resurrection by faith, he remained foreign."[*]

*Luke 24:17

*Luke 24:18

*En ev Luke 24:13-24; PG 123:1114D

*Com Luke 24:18; PL 92:626A

When Jesus asked them what had happened in Jerusalem (not, of course, because he did not know, but so that he could converse with them), *they said: "Concerning Jesus of Nazareth, who was a prophet, mighty in work and word before God and all the people."*[*] And they described how he had been handed over to

*Luke 24:19

death and crucified. Again, Bede: "They acknowledge him to be a prophet, but they say nothing about the Son of God. This may be because they did not yet fully believe, or because they were afraid of falling into the hands of Jesus' enemies: they did not know who this man was, so they were concealing the truth they believed."* They went on to say that they had been hoping that he would be Israel's redeemer, but they had practically lost all hope. This was because it was now the third day since these things had happened: he had predicted he would rise again; the third day was nearly over and he had not appeared to the disciples. Then they added that some of their number had gone to the tomb and come back with disturbing news. They did not report that Christ was risen, but that his body was gone and could not be found, which frightened the disciples.

*Com Luke 24:18; PL 92:626B

Then the Lord took them to task for their response, saying, "*O foolish* in intellectual blindness *and slow of heart* in lack of affection *to believe in all things, which the prophets have spoken* about the Messiah's death and resurrection! *Ought not Christ to have suffered these things*—because it was preordained by the Father, or because in this way Christ could be exalted, or because in this way the human race would be redeemed, or because in this way the Scriptures would be fulfilled—*and so, to enter into his glory*, since it is only by the passion that one can attain this glory?" *Then he expounded to them in all the scriptures the things that were concerning him.* By citing various passages and opening up their hidden meaning in a way sufficient to prove his point, he showed them that all these events had been predicted about him. The foundation of faith is that nothing happened to Christ that had not been foretold.

*Luke 24:25-27

Pause here to consider the Lord's great kindness and goodness. First of all, his fervent love could not

bear to have his own people so mistaken and sad.
Truly the Lord is a faithful friend, a kind and devoted
companion: he walks with them, asks the cause of
their sorrow, and enkindles their hearts by explaining the Scriptures to them. He does the same for us
spiritually each and every day. If we are burdened
by doubt or depression and speak lovingly with him
about it, he is present immediately, comforting and
enlightening our hearts and inflaming them with
his love. The best remedy for such confusing feelings is to speak about God or to think about him.
Following the example of these disciples, we should
converse about God's saving work as we walk down
the road so that Christ will be our companion—and
not only our companion, but also our teacher, just as
he accompanied these two disciples and revealed the
meaning of the Scriptures to them.

It is good to speak about Jesus in all circumstances
and places and to have him always in your thoughts,
because, as we have just seen, he never forgets those
who are mindful of him. He promised, *"Where there
are two or three gathered together in my name, there am
I in the midst of them."** The Lord walks most closely
with those who speak about his passion, because the
recollection of all he suffered for our sake is most
pleasing to him. He has admonished us particularly
about this, saying, *"Remember my poverty,* as a remedy
for greed; *and transgression,* to counteract the hunger
for honors; *the wormwood and the gall,* to resist luxu-
rious living."**

*Matt 18:20

*Lam 3:19

Second, contemplate Christ's goodness not only
as an expression of his love but also of his profound
humility. See how humbly the Lord of all creation
walks alongside his disciples, as if he were just one
of them. Does this not strike you as a return to the
very origin of God's condescension? And a further
sign of his humility is that he did not think it beneath

him to travel and speak in this familiar way with these unimportant disciples who were not numbered among the apostles. This is so unlike those conceited types who will mingle only with the high and mighty. Likewise, if you watch these arrogant people you will notice how patronizing they are: they refuse to use any big words when speaking to the common people because they think it is a waste of breath; such folk are incapable of understanding their so-called advanced ideas. Yet here the Lord shares his mysteries with two ordinary men and does not consider this small company beneath him—he did not disdain to speak like this with even one person, as for example with the Samaritan woman at the well.

Third, consider the Lord's kindness: see how he instructed his disciples, consoled them with his words, and restored them by leading them to belief. He said, *"O foolish and slow of heart to believe in all things,"* * and so on. It is as if he is saying to us, *"O foolish and slow of heart to believe: O foolish and slow of heart* when it comes to searching out the commandments and the will of God! *O foolish and slow of heart* in deepening this knowledge and putting it into practice!" *Luke 24:25

Therefore, let us humble ourselves so that we can truly explore the meaning of God's word and live as it teaches. Let us also humble ourselves when we endure suffering because, if we are made sharers in Christ's passion, we are able also to share in his resurrection and glorification. Whoever does not suffer with him will not enter into that glory that brings about both the knowledge and the fulfillment of God's will. Bede teaches, "Here we learn that if we want to understand the meaning of any passage of Scripture, we must humble ourselves for two reasons: first, to understand what it teaches us, and second, to enable us to put into practice what we have learned. If Moses and the prophets all spoke about Christ and foretold that it was through his bitter passion that he would enter into his glory, on what basis can people boast that they are Christians if they neither devote some little energy to discovering how the Scriptures refer to Christ nor seek to attain the glory they desire to share with Christ by the path of tribulation and suffering?"*

*Com Luke 24:25; PL 92:626D

Christ entered into his glory by passing through the narrow gate of his passion and death to show us that *through many tribulations we must enter into the kingdom of God.*[*] They are foolish and mad who presume to enter into any other kind of glory without suffering and tribulation. Since Christ himself did not enter into a kingdom that was his by nature without great anguish, how much more must we, who can lay claim to this realm only by grace, have to bear with many trials to enter into the kingdom of heaven?

*Acts 14:22

All of Christ's elect and dear ones provide examples—they all came to the reign of God through the path of voluntary suffering. Bernard writes, "We see our head entering heaven through torment and affliction, and we his members dream about finding some other path there! It would be very strange to see the head going through one gate and the body through another; it is shameful to find the members avid for delights while the head is crowned with thorns."* Just as legatees inherit both the obligations and the gifts of a bequest, so God has linked the burden of trials to the inheritance of eternal life. Christ himself bore this burden, as he himself says here: *"Ought not Christ to have suffered these things and so to enter into his glory?"**

*Sermo 5 in Festo Omn Sanct (partial); PL 183:480C

*Luke 24:26

The apostles in turn bore this burden, for they endured persecution for Christ, as he had foretold they would. And all the faithful take up this burden, as the apostle teaches: *"All that live godly in Christ Jesus shall suffer persecution."** Those who want to avoid

*2 Tim 3:12

suffering and attain eternal happiness think they are worthier than Christ, holier than the apostles, and better than all the faithful.

Jesus Joins the Disciples for a Meal

And they drew near to the town where they were going, and the Lord himself *made as though he would go farther,* in order to increase their desire so that they would invite him to stay with them. Bernard observes, "He pretended *he would go farther,* not because he wanted to, but because he wanted to hear, '*Stay with us, because it is toward evening.*'" Wanting to hear more from him, *they constrained him* by taking hold of him, and with gentle and persuasive words they urged him to remain, *saying: "Stay with us, because it is toward evening and the day is now far spent,* and the sun is setting." One lesson here, according to Gregory, is that strangers should not be simply invited to accept hospitality, but even be persuaded with insistence. It would be fitting for someone to say these words when he is near death and the evening or sunset of his life approaches, and with his heart and his lips to invite the Lord to remain with him.

At length he went in with them. And it came to pass, while he was at table with them, he took bread and blessed and broke and gave to them. Watch carefully how Jesus graciously goes in with them in response to their invitation and urging, how they prepare the table and set out the food, how he himself takes the bread and blesses it, how with his own most sacred hands he breaks the bread and gives it to them, acting as he had done before the passion, when it was customary for him to bestow such courteous attention on his own. This was the way he revealed himself to them, because then their spiritual eyes were opened and they knew him by the way he broke the bread.

*Luke 24:28

*SC 74.3; PL 183:1140B

*Luke 24:29

*40 hom 23.1; PL 76:1182D

*Luke 24:30

*Luke 24:31

Scripture records several occasions on which he blessed and broke bread in this way: first, at the multiplication of the five loaves; second, at the distribution of the seven loaves; third, at the consecration of his body; fourth, in this illumination of the disciples. Augustine writes, "We would not be wrong to assume that Satan was the author of this impediment to their eyes, to keep them from recognizing Jesus, but Christ himself had permitted this up until the mystery* of the bread, so that the impediment imposed by the enemy is removed by participating in the unity of his Body, and it is possible to recognize Christ." * And Theophylact says, "He also implies another thing, that the eyes of those who receive the sacred bread are opened so that they can recognize Christ, for the Lord's flesh has in it a great and ineffable power." *

The Lord will act invisibly in our souls daily as he once did for these disciples if we invite him to stay with us and cling to him with our desires, our prayers, and our holy meditations. As the Lord has taught, *we ought always to pray and not lose heart.* And he also does this for our instruction, so that we will make the effort to carry out works of charity, assistance, and hospitality: it is not enough to read or listen to divine words; we must put them into practice. The Lord was not recognized while he was speaking, but when the disciples gave him something to eat. The loving and merciful Lord shows compassion to the compassionate and strengthens their faith. From this incident we are able to know that *faith without works is dead.*

The disciples did not recognize the Lord when they saw him, or even when they heard him interpret and explain the Scriptures, but as soon as they carried out what the Scriptures command, *they knew him in the breaking of bread.* They were not enlightened by hearing the Scriptures and the divine precepts; it

*sacramentum

*De cons ev 3.25.72; PL 34:1206

*En ev Luke 24:25-35; PG 123:1119A

*Luke 18:1

*Jas 2:20

*Luke 24:35

was by doing what the word of God says—welcoming the stranger and feeding him—that they came to understand. As the apostle says, *"For not the hearers of the law are just before God, but the doers of the law shall be justified."* So you will come to know God better by performing acts of kindness and mercy, such as extending hospitality and similar deeds, than by simply reading, explaining, and arguing about the Scriptures. Truth is understood better by doing than by hearing and shows itself more plainly in deeds than in words.

*Rom 2:13

We are all pilgrims in this world, because *we have not here a lasting city, but we seek one that is to come.* If we possess in a spiritual way what these two travelers had, the Lord will be the companion on our journey. They exerted themselves: they walked, they wept, they talked about Christ. So Christ himself joined them, inflamed their hearts, opened the Scriptures to them, and made as if to travel on farther. He will do the same for us, if we rouse ourselves in the face of boredom, mourn to counteract superficial happiness, and speak about Christ rather than engaging in idle chatter. Then Christ will join us, inflame our hearts, teach us the meaning of the Scriptures, and pretend to be going on farther to test us.

*Heb 13:14

Again, as a pilgrim you should rid yourself of everything that is not essential for the journey, search for the right road, hunger with your whole heart for your homeland, and keep your eyes and your heart from wandering to anything that will distract you on your pilgrimage. Be this kind of pilgrim, and Christ will appear to you. And he will do the same three things for you that he did for those two disciples: he will make the time pass quickly with his delightful conversation, he will show you the right path by giving you true understanding, and, finally, he will restore your affectionate love by blessing and breaking bread.

Then, should he act as if he were going on ahead, you can compel him to stay with you.

The Lord did not allow those disciples to enjoy his great bounty for long; as soon as he gave them the bread, *he vanished out of their sight.* He did this to test their affection, and at the same time he showed them that he had a glorified body because he was able to disappear immediately. He had humbled himself to appear to their bodily eyes in a condition of weakness so that the glory of the resurrection could dawn in their minds. Once they were convinced that he had risen, *they said one to the other: "was not our heart burning within us* with ardent love, *while he spoke in the way and opened to us the scriptures?"* Why did we not cling to him? Why did we not throw ourselves at his feet? Why did we not believe what our own hearts were telling us? Where can we seek him? Where can we find him?"

This suggests, according to Origen, that the words spoken by the Savior had filled the hearts of his hearers with divine love. Gregory says, "The mind is set ablaze when the words are heard, the numbness of cold recedes, and the heart spurns earthly delights and becomes solicitous in its desire for spiritual blessings. It gladly listens to heavenly precepts and is instructed by the commandments as if it were set ablaze by many torches." There was another reason that Jesus vanished quickly from their sight: so that they would hurry off to share with others the consolation they themselves had received, as will be seen in the next chapter.

Luke 24:31

Luke 24:32

Theophylact, En ev Luke 24:25-35; PG 123:1119A

40 hom 30.5; PL 76:1223C

> *O Lord Jesus Christ, you appeared to the disciples on their way to Emmaus and inflamed their hearts with your love. Enlighten my heart, I beg you, so that I may fulfill the desires of your counsel with a joyful spirit. May I cleanse myself from all malicious deeds and perform works of mercy and loving kindness. Then, in the*

future resurrection, may I delight to hear those words you will address to all your elect: "Come, blessed of my Father, inherit the Kingdom prepared for you from the foundation of the world." O, only-begotten Son of God, may I hear those sweet words! Amen.

9

Christ Appears in the Upper Room
When Thomas Is Absent

Luke 24:36-47; John 20:19-25

And rising up, the same hour, the two disciples *went back to Jerusalem·* to the disciples who were behind locked doors, for fear of the Jews. According to Theophylact, "Their hearts were set on fire by the Lord's words, so they realized who he was. Therefore they rejoiced and headed back to Jerusalem without a moment's delay."· See the fervor of faith in these disciples, and how anxious they are to reveal the resurrection! Nothing can keep them from proclaiming the Lord's resurrection to the apostles: not the lateness of the hour or the meal or their exhaustion or fear of Jesus' enemies; they hurry back with all their energy to share what they have learned on the road.

·Luke 24:33

·En ev Luke 24:25-35; PG 123:1118A

The disciples went to the Upper Room below Mount Sion, and *they found the eleven* gathered together behind closed doors for fear of the Jews and because of joy at the Lord's resurrection, *and those* others from among the seventy-two *that were with them*, conversing with one another and *saying: "The Lord is risen indeed and has appeared to Simon."·* And, to add even greater certainty to the fact of the resurrection, *they told what things were done in the way*, and how Jesus had appeared to them, *and how they knew him in the breaking of bread.·*

·Luke 24:33-34

·Luke 24:35

The Lord Appears to the Apostles

But some of those present did not believe either the two disciples or the others, and Thomas was one of these. Imagine how much joy filled the room as first one witness and then another announced the good news. While they were sharing their stories, Thomas slipped out of the room. When he had left, and the disciples were talking about what they had heard and seen, *it was late the same day, the first of the week*, that is, the day of the Lord's resurrection, *and the doors were shut where the disciples were gathered together for fear of the Jews.** But the doors were also locked according to God's plan, so that by passing through them Jesus could reveal to his followers the power of his virtue and the nature of his glorified body. *John 20:19

Drawn to his disciples by their great desire, *Jesus came and stood in the midst** of them, resplendent in white robes and the freshness of his resurrection. He could be seen by them all because they were gathered together in his name. He appeared to them when they were together, and the Holy Spirit likewise descended on them gathered together, because Christ and the Holy Spirit are only to be found where people are brought together in charity. Christ *stood in the midst* of the disciples: like the sun among stars, so he could illuminate them; like a blossom among the lilies, so he could adorn them; like a leader among his troops, so he could rally them; like a teacher among his pupils, so he could instruct them; like a father among his children, so he could unite them; like a heart among the members of the body, so he could vivify them, and as the friend of all, so that he could unite himself with each of them. *John 20:19

Here you should meditate on the fact that the Lord came to stand in the midst of those who were speaking about him, from which we learn that we will have him in our midst as well if, whenever we come together, we do those things that pertain to his glory and our welfare. As he himself said, *"Where there are two or three gathered together in my name, there am I in the midst of them."** *Matt 18:20

When Jesus the Savior came to the disciples, they were afraid, night had fallen, they were together, and the doors were closed. These circumstances teach us that four things are necessary if we hope to welcome the Savior into our midst. The first is holy fear, which sweeps clean the home of our conscience, as we read in the book of Ecclesiasticus: *The fear of the Lord drives out sin, for he that is without fear cannot be justified.*[1]*

*Sir 1:27-28

The second is disregard for ostentatious display, which is signified by the fact that the Lord comes to us at night, when the light of worldly attractions has been extinguished and we disdain such things with all our heart. The third is unity, because they were gathered together in charity, and the Savior does not visit those who are quarreling, as the apostle teaches: *"Have peace, and the God of grace and of love shall be with you."** The fourth is stability, by which you abide in the home of your conscience, not allowing your curiosity to cause you to wander after things outside: keep the doors of your senses closed, and wait in this way for the Savior.

*2 Cor 13:11

*John 20:19

Then *Jesus said to them: "Peace be to you."** By this he did not mean external peace, because they were to experience many trials; rather, he meant peace of heart in the present and eternal peace hereafter. *He said to them: "Peace be to you"* because he was announcing their reconciliation with God, because he was commanding them to safeguard charity and unity, and because he was promising to give them the peace of eternal life. He extended peace because he had come for the sake of peace. It is beautiful to see that the first thing the Lord does after rising from the dead is to recommend peace to his disciples, in order to show that he allows those who foster peace

---

[1] The Vulgate differs from the Septuagint and modern translations.

and harmony to see him. From this it is obvious that peacemakers are truly Christ's disciples. Chrysostom suggests that he said *"Peace be to you"* to the men because they were to be constantly at war with their enemies among the Jews, but that his first gift to the women was joy, because their great burden was their sorrow. So the good news announced to the men was peace in the face of war, and to the women joy in the face of sorrow.[*] Then, to assure the disciples that it was not someone else and that they were not seeing a ghost, he added, *"It is I, that is, myself in person; not something imaginary or an illusion of the devil; fear not,[*] nor doubt."*

*Hom John 86.3; PG 59:470

*Luke 24:36

The Risen Christ Can Be Touched, and He Eats

But being troubled by the wonder and marvel of it, *and frightened* by the natural fear felt by the living in the presence of the dead, *they supposed that they saw a spirit*[*] that Jesus had sent forth at the end of his passion and were not beholding him in the flesh. They did not yet believe that a body could rise after three days in the tomb, or that a resurrected body could pass through closed doors. Divine Providence allowed them to doubt so that our faith would have greater evidence of the Lord's resurrection. *And he said to them: "Why are you troubled, and why do thoughts arise from* the false and fantastic depths of *your* weak and wavering *hearts,*[*] rather than descending from the true and good heights of heaven?"*

*Luke 24:37

*Luke 24:38

And since faith could still harbor doubts when only seeing his body, he showed them his hands, his feet, and his pierced side, which could be touched, in order to demonstrate his bodily resurrection. In this way he declared that he who had been crucified, had died, and had been pierced by the lance had risen again in the same body. *"See my hands and feet,"* he

*Luke 24:39 said; *"It is I myself."** This was as much as to say, "By
these scars you will recognize that I who have risen
am he who had died. The enduring wounds show
that this is my same body. The resurrection is true:
the very same body has risen." *Handle, and see, for a*
Luke 24:39 spirit has not flesh and bones, as you see me to have. Jesus
retained the marks of his wounds in order to heal
their questioning hearts; he showed them his scars
to heal the wounds of their doubt and lack of faith.

*Luke 24:40   *And when he had said this, he showed them his hands**
to rouse them to battle. He was saying, "Look at these
hands that fought for you—I show them to you so
that you, too, will fight, because you will not be victorious unless you struggle. Act bravely, because *to*
him that shall overcome, I will give to sit with me on my
*Rev 3:21   throne."** *He showed them his side** to enkindle their
*John 20:20 love. He was saying, "Behold this open side and
pierced heart, so that you may see how much I have
loved you, and so you will also love me." *He showed*
*Luke 24:40 them his feet** to encourage them to persevere. May
we not turn back once we have taken the good path!
This is what perseverance means: when neither fear
nor love, convenience nor inconvenience can turn any
away from living a godly life, keeping the commandments, or fulfilling a vow they have made.

      Five principal demons assail us, and we must
struggle to fend them off. The first is the attachment
to sins, unjust things, carnal pleasures, or worldly
honors; this is strong in some hearts and leads to
the loss of heavenly glory. The second is the fear en-
gendered by a lack of trust: this afflicts those who
think that God does not want to help them persevere in doing good or undertaking a demanding
penance—when instead they will endure an even
harsher penance in Gehenna. The third is pining for
worldly or carnal delights that must be forsaken or
have already been renounced. O poor one, what are

you doing? You prefer sickness to health, death to life, sorrow to joy, eternal suffering to glory. The fourth is discomfiture about doing good, when we think that others will make fun of us if we wear shabby clothes, fast, pray, make a pilgrimage, or undertake similar practices. The fifth is the false hope that causes some to say, "God is merciful. He will not condemn us for these trifles; besides, we are Christians." This kind of hope crumbles to ruins. Hope is the sure expectation of future blessings on the basis of one's just deserts: people like this have produced no good fruit, so they are not really hopeful—they are presumptuous.

The fact that he offered his body to be touched was something miraculous, because the Lord's body is incorrupt and immortal, and it is impossible in the natural course of things for a body possessing these qualities to be handled by those who are mortal and subject to corruption. In a wondrous and ineffable way, Gregory says, he allowed his body to be handled in order to restore our faith, and he showed that it was incorrupt to attract us to the prize. By showing that he could be touched and was incorruptible, he demonstrated that he had the same nature as before the passion, that is, he truly had a human body, but it now possessed a different kind of glory: his same human body was now incorruptible.*

*40 hom 26.1; PL 76:1198A

And because the general resurrection is prefigured by the Lord's resurrection, he wants us to understand that after the resurrection our bodies will be endowed by divine power with incorruptibility in such a way that they can be touched by other bodies of a similar kind. Our flesh will be raised up in its true nature, but without corruption or the infirmity of death. Bede writes, "It would not have been enough for him to let them see him with their eyes, if he had not allowed them also to touch him with their hands. By allowing the disciples to touch his flesh and bones,

*Com Luke
24:39; PL
92:629C

*Matt 13:43

*De civ Dei
22.19.2; PL
41:781

*Luke 24:42

he showed quite openly the true state of resurrection—a condition that he enjoys now and we will
enjoy in the future."* Augustine, however, makes
this point: "The brightness with which *the just shine
as the sun in the kingdom of their Father* must have been
concealed from the eyes of the disciples in Christ's
risen body. Do not think it was absent; rather, feeble
human eyesight could not bear it, and it was necessary for them to be able to look upon him so they
could recognize him."*

And, since some of them still doubted, he asked
them if they had anything to eat, so that by taking
food he might add an even more convincing proof of
the resurrection. *And they offered him a piece of a broiled
fish and a honeycomb.*² These were most appropriate
things to offer him: he himself was like the broiled
fish on account of the suffering of his human nature,
and like the honeycomb in the sweetness of his divine
nature. The honeycomb is also a good image of the
two natures in the one Person of Christ: the honey is
contained in the wax, and his divinity—the sweetness
of his divine nature—is contained in his humanity.
The two foods offered to the Lord also suggest what
we also should offer him: bodily mortification, symbolized by the broiled fish, and spiritual devotion,
symbolized by the honeycomb.

Or perhaps the Lord wanted his food to be broiled
fish accompanied by honeycomb because, like a fish,
he was hidden beneath the surface of the waters of his
human generation; the waters were stirred up, and he
was caught in the net of human death, broiled by the

² The honeycomb does not appear in many Greek manuscripts
and is omitted in modern translations. It is cited, however, by
many fathers of the church, both Latin and Greek, as far back as a
work attributed to Justin, *De Resurrectione*, chap. 9, and Tertullian,
De Corona, chap. 14 (PL 2:100A).

fire and tribulation of the passion, and cooked on the altar of the cross. But he who had been like a broiled fish in his passion emerged like the honeycomb in his resurrection, and sweeter to us than honey itself. So those who maintain faith in the passion and resurrection offer Christ both broiled fish and honeycomb. Theophylact suggests that the broiled fish stands for the active life, which dries up our moisture on the coals of labor, while the honeycomb represents the contemplative life, on account of the sweetness of God's utterances.*

*En ev Luke 24:36-44; PG 123:1122D

Jesus did not eat from a need for earthly food. Bede says, "In order to demonstrate the truth of his resurrection the Lord deigned not only to be touched by his disciples but also to eat with them. This is not because he needed food, nor as if we should expect that we will need to eat in our resurrected state, but to show that he had truly risen bodily; otherwise, they might have judged that he had no body and was simply a spirit, and thought the apparition to be not real, but imaginary."*

*Com Luke 24:43; PL 92:631A

In a literal sense, Jesus gave them three proofs of his resurrection: first, by sight, saying, *"See my hands and feet, it is I myself"*; second, by touch, saying, *"Handle, and see: for a spirit has not flesh and bones, as you see me to have"*; and third by taste, when he asked, *"Have you here anything to eat?"* In a spiritual sense, those who meditate on the Lord's resurrection see Christ risen; those who unite themselves to him in charity touch and handle him; those who endure the fires of tribulation for the sake of his name offer him broiled fish; and those who lavish works of charity on the members of his Body give him honeycomb.

*And when he had eaten before them, taking the remains of the food, he gave to them.** He did this either to show that he had really eaten some of the food or to suggest that they should imitate his passion, which is bitter

*Luke 24:43

because of bodily suffering but most sweet in the reward it gives. Those who are roasted here below like
fish for the sake of truth will be satisfied in heaven
with the honeycomb of everlasting sweetness.

Then he gave evidence of his resurrection through
hearing, saying, *"These are the words which I spoke to
you* (such as, *'Behold we go up to Jerusalem,* etc.*') while
I was yet with you* in the flesh before my passion, *that
all things must needs be fulfilled* in the event *which are
written in the law of Moses and in the prophets and in the
psalms concerning me."* These three writings signify
the entire Old Testament.

*Luke 24:44

Christ Reveals the Meaning of the Scriptures to His Disciples

Then with an inner grace *he opened their understanding,* which had hitherto been closed, *that they
might understand the scriptures,* in order to know
about his resurrection from them. Just as he had
demonstrated the truth of his resurrection so far as
his humanity was concerned, now he did so as regards his divinity, for to illuminate immediately the
minds of the ignorant as to the meaning of Scripture
is a property of divinity itself. Before the passion he
had declared that he was true God and true Man,
and he did so again after his resurrection. *And he said
to them,* to instruct them by his teaching, *"Thus it is
written."* (In other words, "You should well believe
it, because it was written that thus it would happen,
and it happened as it was written.") And he went
on, *"And thus it was proper for Christ to suffer and to
rise again from the dead, the third day."* *It was proper,* or
necessary, not for Christ, but for us: his passion was
not needed for his sake, but to free us from the debt
we owed, and by means of his holy resurrection to
show us how we could reign with him.

*Luke 24:45

*Luke 24:46

Rightly the apostle teaches, *Christ died for our sins* and rose again for our justification.* He opened the Scriptures to them: then the Lamb that had been slain *has prevailed to open the book and* by the Spirit of divinity *to loose the seven seals thereof.* These seven seals are the mysteries of Christ's incarnation, baptism, preaching, works, passion, resurrection, and ascension. This makes it clear that the meaning of Sacred Scripture will never be properly grasped unless *he that has the key of David, he that opens and no man shuts,* opens it.

*1 Cor 15:3
*Rom 4:25

*Rev 5:5

*Rev 3:7

The reason that Jesus chose to die and rise again for us, as was just said, is made clear by what he says next: *"And that penance* on the part of men and women *and remission of sins* on the part of God, who alone can forgive sins, *should be preached in his name, unto all nations,* and not just to the Jewish people or in one part of the world." Having demonstrated the truth of his bodily presence, Christ goes on to point out the unity of the church. According to Theophylact, it no longer pleased God to have the human race divided into Jews and Gentiles.* The preaching of Jesus, of John the Baptist before him, and of the apostles after him all began with a call to repentance for the forgiveness of sins, and, lest any think that they cannot be forgiven because of the gravity of their sin, Jesus adds, *"beginning at Jerusalem."* Jerusalem is the center of the inhabited world, so it was fitting that the proclamation of the Gospel should begin from there, and as Christ's disciples dispersed throughout the world, the voice of their preaching would resound everywhere.

*Luke 24:47

*En ev Luke
24:45-53; PG
123:1126A

*Luke 24:47

Hence Theophylact goes on to say that Christ commanded his followers to begin their preaching in Jerusalem and end it among the Gentiles, so that he might unite all people in one.* Nor should any feel that the heinousness of their sins bars the gates of

*En ev Luke
24:45-53; PG
123:1126A

forgiveness to them; let them recall the mercy shown to Jerusalem itself, the city where lying voices and cruel hands brought about the shedding of the blood that redeemed the world. According to Bede, they began from Jerusalem so that the Gentiles who were enmeshed in various errors might be moved to have hope chiefly by this sign of divine mercy: that mercy was extended to the very ones who had crucified the Son of God.* And Chrysostom writes, "The disciples displayed the signs of his resurrection first among his murderers themselves, in the very city where the outrage of his death was perpetrated, so that no one could say that the disciples had abandoned their own kin and gone off to show themselves to strangers. Where the executioners themselves appear as believers, there the resurrection is most fully demonstrated."*

Before his passion, Christ had told his disciples, *"I will see you again and your heart shall rejoice."** This had now come to pass, which is why Scripture says that *the disciples therefore were glad, when they saw* (that is, recognized) *the Lord.** Those who had been downcast, and then terrified, were now made joyful by the consolation of his presence. And who would not rejoice at the sight of such loving kindness? *He showed them his hands* pierced by the nails, his *hands* that had won salvation in the midst of the earth; his *feet*, tired out by walking on the roads as he went about preaching; his *side*, from which he had caused the sacraments of redemption to flow. Jesus had kept the marks of the wounds in all these places to heal the hearts of those who doubted. Confronted with the emblems of such mercy, *the disciples therefore were glad when they saw the Lord*, because, having seen him, they could not help but rejoice.

*He said therefore to them again: "Peace be to you."** He said *"Peace"* again because of the twofold com-

*Com Luke 24:47; PL 92:632B

*Hom Acta 1.4; PG 60:20

*John 16:22

*John 20:20

*John 20:21

mandment: love of God and neighbor. Those who have twofold charity preserve this twofold peace. Or he repeated this greeting because *he is our peace, who has made both one.** Or again, he gave this greeting twice to show that through his blood he had made peace both on earth and in the heavens. It was as if he said, *"Peace I leave with you,* that is, traces of peace in your hearts at present; *my peace I give unto you,* that is, everlasting peace in the world to come. I reiterate this greeting to show you that you are reconciled with God, and with the angels, and with one another." In this way, we may love God and love one another for God's sake. According to John Chrysostom, at the same time this greeting shows the power of the cross, which sweeps away all sorrow and confers every blessing; this is true peace.*

*Eph 2:14

*Hom John 86.3; PG 59:470

The Gift of the Holy Spirit

Then Jesus added, *"As the Father has sent me* to teach in Judea, *I also* will *send you** to announce this truth to the whole world. I constitute you as my vicars, I send you in my place, I entrust my office to you: *I send you* to teach, to preach, to baptize, and to glorify my name and my Father's name." He showed himself to be our mediator when he said *he sent me* and *I send you:* the Father sent his Son when he appointed him to become incarnate, and the Son sent the apostles when he commissioned them to proclaim this same incarnation throughout the whole world. And just as the Father who loved the Son sent him into the world to endure great suffering and tribulation for the salvation of believers, so the Son who loved the apostles sent them to bear with evils and torments for the sake of his name. Pope Gregory writes, "Therefore he says, *'As the Father has sent me, I also send you':* when I send you into the midst of the

*John 20:21

offenses of your persecutors, I am loving you with that love by which the Father loved me when he sent me to endure tribulation."*

*40 hom 26.2; PL 76:1198B

Because the fulfillment of this office cannot be carried out suitably without the grace of the Holy Spirit, *when he had said this, he breathed on them; and he said to them: "Receive the Holy Spirit."** He imparted the Holy Spirit by breathing on them to show that he himself had breathed the breath of life into the first man, or to show clearly that the Holy Spirit proceeds from him just as he proceeds from the Father. Augustine teaches, "That bodily breath was not the substance of the Holy Spirit, but an indication by a fitting sign that the Holy Spirit does not proceed from the Father alone, but also from the Son."*

*John 20:22
*De Trin 4.20.29; PL 42:908

The forgiveness of sins is attributed to the Holy Spirit because this is the fruit and effect of the Spirit, so quite rightly Jesus then says to the disciples to whom he has given the Spirit, *Whose sins you shall forgive, they are forgiven them; and whose sins you shall retain, they are retained.* Here he empowers them to bind and to loose—not by their own personal power, but as ministers of the church. Augustine says, "To make it even more clear that the forgiveness of sins is attributed to the Holy Spirit whom he has given to the faithful and not to human merit, he immediately adds, 'Whose sins you shall forgive, they are forgiven them,' that is, the Spirit forgives, not you; the Spirit is God, and God forgives, not you. It is God dwelling in his holy temple, among his holy faithful, who forgives sins through the church's ministers, who are living temples."* It is true that God alone forgives sin in the first place, but the church's ministers do so sacramentally through the power of the keys, although only for those who are within the communion of the church. For this reason, the same Augustine says, "The church's charity, which is poured into our hearts

*John 20:23
*Sermo 90.9; PL 38:600

by the Holy Spirit, forgives the sins of those who are part of her but retains the sins of those who are not."* You can perceive how all these events overflowed with rejoicing and happiness and what a joyful Pasch this was! How blessed that little room was, and how glorious to be dwelling there!

*Tr John ev 121.4; PL 35:1958

Three spiritual lessons can be drawn from this appearance of the Lord, which the faithful soul should strive to ponder when in the presence of the eternal Word. The first is that the soul should leave off all external work, as is suggested by the fact that this appearance took place on the Sabbath, the day of rest, when the Jews did not work. The second is that we should safeguard the senses from all distractions, signified by the closed doors; the doors of the soul are the bodily senses and the spiritual powers. The third is that all our attention should be focused on interior recollection, which is symbolized by the disciples' being gathered together in one place; the powers of the soul are like disciples, gathered together under the teaching authority of the eternal Word.

When Jesus comes into a soul he does five things. First, he stands in the midst of all the disciples, that is, the soul's faculties, in which he takes up his dwelling, and with his grace he perfects and fructifies the essence of that soul and all its powers, bestowing divine life. Second, he announces peace to the disciples. Notice to whom he proclaims peace: to those who are his disciples. May you also be an attentive disciple, able to receive Christ's discipline. Third, he shows them his hands and his side, conferring on them divine actions, signified by his hands, and divine affections, symbolized by his side, beneath which his heart lies hidden. Fourth, he causes the disciples to rejoice, imparting to them an interior joy; *the disciples were glad when they saw the Lord.* Fifth, he breathes on them, bestowing the life-giving Spirit, so that they might live for the good of their own salvation and that of others.

The Lord Departs; Thomas Returns

The Lord did not remain with them long, because it was indeed late in the evening. But they coaxed him to linger with them for a while, asking him not to leave so soon; nor did this displease the Lord, for he enjoyed being with them. Finally, with a blessing he parted from them. When he had gone, Thomas, who had left before the Lord appeared, came back. With joyful hearts, *the other disciples therefore said* the glad tidings *to him: "We have seen the Lord."*˙ Thomas said he would not believe unless he saw with his own eyes and could also touch the scars of his wounds; in that way, if sight was deceived, touch would confirm the truth. He demanded that evidence be submitted to the tribunal of the two senses least easily deceived: sight and touch. Having seen Jesus suffer such death torments, he could not accept any arguments that he was risen and alive unless he could not only see but also touch. Chrysostom writes, "Being coarser than the others, he sought to believe by means of the coarsest sense, the sense of touch; he would not even believe his eyes."˙ The disciples hungered to see their Lord again and thirsted for his presence; formerly they had been accustomed to such abundance from him, and repeatedly they begged him with longing sighs to return.

˙John 20:25

˙Hom John 87.1; PG 59:473

Recapitulation of the Appearances on Easter Day

You have seen how all five of these appearances took place on Easter day. Perhaps you have heard and not been moved, because you did not enter wholeheartedly into the Lord's passion. But I believe that

if you knew how to enter into the passion by your
compassion, with your mind concentrated on it—not
dissipated by worldly, superfluous, or captivating
trivialities—you would be able to experience these
appearances as if every Sunday were Easter. Every
Friday and Saturday would plunge you into his passion, as the apostle says: *"As you are partakers of the
sufferings, so shall you be also of the consolation."* *

*2 Cor 1:7

Then the Lord Jesus returned to the holy ancestors, who were not idle in his presence: they continuously sang his praises with great jubilation. All those
holy ancestors, joined by the angelic host, reverently,
devoutly, and joyfully rejoiced before him with songs
and canticles. Watch them and join in their celebration; learn how to praise and worship God, to give
him thanks and bless him for his benefits. Do not
cease to glorify him with your whole heart, so that
you may continually sing praises in his presence with
such a noble multitude.

> *O beloved Son of God the Father, you appeared to your
> disciples when they were gathered together behind
> locked doors. Close the inner and outer gates of my
> senses against the dangers of temptation by a rever-
> ent and holy fear of you. Put all wickedness to death
> in them with the gentle fetters of your charity, and
> illumine them with the light of divine religion, so that
> I may deserve to be consoled by the joy of seeing you.
> May I find, by your gift, peace of heart here and hereaf-
> ter, so that with your angels and all the holy elect I may
> deserve to praise you worthily without ceasing. Amen.*

10

The Lord Appears Again, with Thomas Present

John 20:26-29

On the octave day of the resurrection the Lord
Jesus appeared once again to his disciples. Because
Thomas was led to doubt out of ignorance, not malice, his kind Master did not want to leave such a well-
loved disciple in unbelief, so he deigned to appear
again in order to restore his faith.

*And after eight days, again his disciples were within,
and Thomas with them. Jesus,* the Good Shepherd who
was solicitous for his little flock, *came, the doors being
shut, and stood in the midst and said, "Peace be to you."*˙
The Lord frequently proclaims peace to his disciples,
commends it to them, and urges them to possess it,
for without peace it is impossible to please God. God
dwells with those who love peace and concord, because *his place is in peace:*˙ on coming into the world he
brought peace, and when he departed from the world
he left his peace behind. The entire perfection of Christian living consists in peace and mutual love, so we
should diligently strive for peace and studiously safeguard it. For this reason, Gregory Nazianzen writes,

˙John 20:26

˙Ps 75:3

> It would be shameful for us to cease attending to
> the work of peace, which Christ bequeathed to
> us when he left the earth. Peace! How sweet the
> word, and the reality! It comes from God, for we
> speak of *the peace of God*; it is an attribute of God,
> for we speak of *the God of peace*. It is in fact God
> himself, as Saint Paul teaches when he says of

Christ, *"He is our peace."** All praise peace—but few pursue it. Why is this? Perhaps from a desire to control others or to amass possessions, or from envy, hatred, or contempt, or some such vice. We would need to ask those who are ignorant of the things of God.*

*Eph 2:14

*Orat 22 de pace; PG 35:1131A

Then he said to Thomas, as if in answer to his earlier demand, *"Put your finger here, and see my hands."** Not that Thomas could see with his finger; rather, it is as if Christ were saying, "Touch here, and find out." *See* in this context is a figure of speech, meaning to realize or understand. We use the word this way in connection with all of our senses: for instance, "Taste this, and see how sweet it is." *Seeing* suggests certitude in relation to each of our five senses. This is why, according to Augustine, the word *see* is commonly used of the other four senses, and in fact it is also used sometimes to mean "understand"—as when you ask someone, "Don't you see?" meaning, "Don't you understand?"**

*John 20:27

*Tr John ev 121.5; PL 35:1958

Or it may be that by responding to Thomas's words Jesus was manifesting his divinity, because he knew what Thomas had said even though he was not present when he said it. Thomas had demanded proof from two of his senses, sight and touch, which is why he said, *"Except I shall see in his hands the print of the nails and put my finger into the place of the nails and put my hand into his side, I will not believe."** This is why Jesus said to him, *"Put your finger* here into the holes *and see my hands** marked by the nails." Then he added, *"And bring your hand here and put it into my side** that was pierced by the lance, so that you may know that I am the same man who was crucified." In a spiritual sense, the finger symbolizes discernment and the hand our works; by inviting us to place our finger and our hand into his sacred wounds, our Lord urges us to bring all of our discernment and works into his service.

*John 20:25

*John 20:27

*John 20:27

*John 20:27   Then Jesus said, *"And be not faithless*, that is, slow to believe, *but believing*,* that is, firm in your faith. Unbelief crucifies me anew, because it was this that brought me to my passion." He said this because, when Thomas was told that Christ had risen, he protested that only by these proofs would he believe it. He had expressed his doubts in the presence of the others, so he was commanded to see and to touch in their presence. John Chrysostom writes, "When you see this incredulous disciple, think about the Lord's mercy: he came for the sake of only one follower and showed him his wounds in order to save him. He did not appear to him immediately, but only after eight days, so that after Thomas heard the other disciples repeatedly giving him their testimony, his desires might

Hom John   be inflamed and he would believe more firmly later."
87.1; PG
59:473   Then Thomas touched the Lord's wounds, and, because we must confess with our lips as well as believe in our hearts in order to be saved, *he answered*

*John 20:28   *and said to him: "My Lord and my God."* That is,

> You are *my Lord* according to your human nature, for by your blood you purchased me and redeemed me, *and my God* according to your divine nature, for you created me and formed me out the clay. No longer do I doubt. I am convinced: I attest to your resurrection, I proclaim your immortality. You are *my Lord* and Master; *I am your servant, and*
> *Ps 115:16   *the son of your handmaid.* Indeed, you are *my God*, who created me, and who became man to redeem me, who gave yourself over to death for my sake, so that you could raise me up to life with you, now that you have risen from the dead. This is my faith; I perceive it, I believe it.

O fortunate Thomas, what blessed license your hand enjoyed! It was indeed a great privilege to be allowed to put your hand into that most sweet and life-giving wounded side: into that side by which we are delivered from wrath, cleansed of our sins, born anew in grace, and raised up to glory.

Thomas is called *Didymus*, Greek for "twin," because of his doubting heart; but his name also means "abyss," because he penetrated the depths of divine mysteries with sure faith.[1] The great recompense faith receives is suggested by what Jesus says next: *"Because you have seen me, Thomas, and ascertained the truth by touching, you have believed: blessed are they that have not seen and have believed."* Not only is Thomas's faith praised in this brief verse, but our future salvation is also predicted. It is as if the Lord were saying, "You are truly blessed, because when you saw me, you believed; but they also will be blessed who, although they do not see me bodily, believe in their hearts." Augustine teaches that Christ used these verbs in the past tense to express certainty: by virtue of his own predestining, he knew things yet to be as if they had already happened; all past and future events are in the present for him.

John 20:29

Thomas saw and touched with his bodily senses, but he believed something different with his heart, because the act of faith must move beyond appearances. As the apostle teaches, *"Faith is the evidence of things that appear not."* He saw and touched the human being who was present and believed him to be the God who could not be seen. By addressing him as *my Lord* he recognized the man Jesus who had been given dominion over all creation; by hailing him as *my God* he confessed him to be the one through whom all things were made, and that the same Christ was both Lord and God. This is why Theophylact says, "He who had formerly been incredulous became the

Tr John ev 121.5; PL 35:1959

Heb 11:1

[1] Jerome interprets *Thomas* as *abyss* or *twin* [PL 23:843]. Jerome, *Liber interpretationum hebraicorum nominum*, CCSL 72 (Turnhout: Brepols Publishers, 1959).

most profound theologian after touching Christ's side, because he clearly professed the two natures united hypostatically to the one Person of Christ."*

It was for our consolation that the Lord added, *"Blessed are they that have not seen and have believed."* Gregory the Great comments, "We rejoice greatly at what follows: *Blessed are they that have not seen and have believed.* Surely these words refer especially to us, who have not seen him in the flesh and yet treasure him in our hearts. But this is true only if good works follow in the wake of our faith; the believer expresses faith in action. Of those who only retain faith in name, Paul says, *'They profess that they know God, but in their works they deny him.'** And James says of them, *'Faith without works is dead.'"**

When someone thinks, "Would that I were alive back then and could see Christ performing miracles," Chrysostom suggests that that one call to mind the words, "Blessed are they that have not seen and have believed."* Thomas's doubting was permitted by divine dispensation, so that the proofs of the Lord's resurrection would be even greater; he doubted so that we would not. Gregory writes,

> This did not happen by chance, but by the working of divine providence. That chosen disciple had been absent earlier. When he heard about the resurrection he doubted; doubting, he touched; and touching, he believed. In this way, the doubts could be banished from our hearts: when he touched the wounds in his Master's body, he healed the wounds of doubt in us. Thomas's unbelief was of greater service to our faith than the belief of the others, because when he was led back to faith by touching, our minds were freed of doubt and confirmed in faith.*

Pope Leo teaches, "It would have been enough for Thomas to see in order to believe; he touched what he

Margin notes:

*En ev John 20:24-29; PG 124:302A

*Titus 1:16
*Jas 2:26; 40 hom 26.9; PL 76:1202B

*Hom John 87.1; PG 59:473

*40 hom 26.7; PL 76:1201C

saw to increase our faith."[*] Gregory, again, has this to say about the reluctance of Thomas and the other disciples to believe: "That the disciples were slow to believe was not due to their weakness; rather, I would say, it was to strengthen us. In the face of their doubt, Jesus showed them many proofs of his resurrection; when we read of these, the result is that we grow strong precisely because of their doubts. Mary Magdalen, who was quick to believe, has helped me less than Thomas, who doubted so stubbornly. He touched the scars of the wounds, and in so doing cut out of our hearts the wound of doubt."[*]

[*]Ps-Maximus of Turin, Sermo 32, Easter Sermon 4; PL 57:599B

[*]40 hom 29.1; PL 76:1568

Why the Risen Christ Retained the Scars of His Wounds

The Lord who had destroyed death's dominion chose to keep the marks of the wounds on his incorrupt body, not because he was powerless to heal them, but to enlighten us about many things. First, to give even more evidence for his resurrection, and to correct and strengthen the faith of his followers in the face of their lingering doubts: he showed them his wounds to prove that the risen Lord was the same man who had been crucified, so that they would believe that he who had been nailed to the cross had risen again in the same body. As he says in Luke's gospel, *"See my hands and feet, that it is I myself."*[*] Second, to show the depth of his love for us, so that when confronted with the signs of the death he endured out of love for us, we in turn would be moved to respond with love to love. We read in the book of Revelation, *who has loved us and washed us from our sins in his own blood.*[*]

[*]Luke 24:39

[*]Rev 1:5

Third, to proclaim our redemption, because his wounds were the sign of our redemption. The prophet Isaiah says, *"He was wounded for our iniquities."*[*] Let

[*]Isa 53:5

all the redeemed never cease to sing the mercies of the Lord: *"Let them say so that have been redeemed by the Lord, for he is good, for his mercy endures forever."* *

*Ps 106:2, 1

Fourth, to instruct and edify us; for if the signs of the passion remained in Christ's glorified body, then we ought to bear them always in our hearts through compassion and give thanks for them. The apostle says, *"Let this mind be in you, which was also in Christ Jesus."* * Fifth, to provide a permanent record, an abiding memorial so that we will never forget how cruelly he was wounded for our sake; as God says through the prophet Isaiah, *"I will not forget you. Behold, I have engraved you in my hands."* *

*Phil 2:5

*Isa 49:15-16

Sixth, to reconcile us with God the Father, who pardons the human race for whose sake the Son willed to be wounded; the apostle writes, *"We have an advocate with the Father, Jesus Christ the just, and he is the propitiation for our sins."* * He pleads on our behalf to the Father, manifesting his obedience and showing eternally the kind of death he endured, which is how he intercedes for us. Bernard says, "You enjoy secure access to God when you have the Son standing before the Father and the Mother standing before the Son. The Son shows the Father his wounds, the Mother shows the Son her breast: who can fear rejection in the presence of such emblems of charity?" *

*1 John 2:1-2

*Arnold, De laud; PL 189:1726D

Seventh, to confound the wicked, who, when they gaze upon these wounds on Judgment Day, will have to concede that they are justly condemned. According to Augustine, the judge will say to those who are condemned, "Behold the man whom you crucified; see the wounds that you inflicted; recognize the side you pierced—it was opened through you and for you, but you refused to enter in." * Eighth, for the joy of the elect, when they will behold by these signs how deep the Lord's love is for them. According to Bede, there will be great rejoicing among the saints when they

*De sym 8.17; PL 40:647

see the wounds gleaming in Christ's flesh, because it was through them that the victor triumphed over the power of death and saved his elect.* When the Lord comes in judgment, he will appear in the same way to the just and the unjust: the just will see how many and how great were the sufferings Christ endured for them, and their love will be even more enkindled; but the unjust will suffer even more and be confounded when it becomes clear how ungrateful they were for so many benefits and how shamefully they despised all God's gifts.

*Source unknown

Ninth, so that Christ's great triumph over the devil might be shown to all creatures and proclaimed through all ages by means of these insignia of his victory. Imagine a soldier who fought courageously to protect his people, receiving many wounds, and who vanquished his enemy, despoiled him, and announced victory to his people. If a physician were to ask him, "Do you wanted to be treated in such a way that all your scars are removed, or do you want the scars to remain?" I think he would choose the latter, because the scars serve as a reminder of his victory and an incentive for others to imitate his courage. So it is with Christ's wounds: they are not a blemish, but an adornment.

Chrysostom says that Christ's wounds are more brilliant than the rays of the sun.* And it is Augustine's opinion that in heaven the wounds that the blessed martyrs received for the sake of Christ's name will still be visible on their bodies, like a star in the heavens, a precious stone in a ring, a flower on its stem, and the scarlet hue on a rose. These marks will be a dignity, not a deformity, and although they will be on the body, theirs will not be merely a bodily comeliness, but the beauty of resplendent virtue.*

*Source unknown

*De civ Dei 22.19.3; PL 41:782

Conclusion

Contemplate now the Lord, and consider his customary gentleness, humility, and fervent love and how he showed his wounds to Thomas and the other disciples to remove all confusion from their hearts, for their benefit and ours. He remained with them for a little while, speaking of the consolations of the kingdom of God; they stood around listening to his words with ineffable delight and gazing upon his face, which was so joyful, beautiful, and gracious. Observe with what friendliness they surround him. You, too, should stand there—at a discrete distance— modestly, reverently, but joyfully too: it may be that, unworthy though you are, he may be moved to invite you to draw closer to him. At length, he instructed them to go to Galilee, where he would appear to them again as he had promised. Giving them a blessing, he departed from them. They stayed there as before, hungering and thirsting for his presence, but greatly consoled.

> *Lord Jesus Christ, you showed doubting Thomas the imprint of the nails and lance and recalled him from error by inviting him to place his finger and hand into your wounds. Grant that I may be ever mindful of your passion and wounds so that I may employ my fingers and hands, that is, my discernment and my actions, completely in your service. With Thomas may I profess that you are my Lord, who purchased me with your blood, and my God, who created me, so that I may be found worthy to experience what you had said about those who would believe in you in the future. Through your great kindness may I be blessed to be found with you. Amen.*

11

The Lord Appears to Seven Disciples by the Sea of Tiberias

John 21:1-25

After an interval, *Jesus showed himself to the disciples at the sea of Tiberias.* *Showed himself* means that Jesus appeared in a visible way to the disciples, for, according to Ambrose, he had the power to be seen or unseen at will.* Seven of the disciples had gone fishing one night for food: *Simon Peter and Thomas, who is called Didymus, and Nathanael, who was of Cana of Galilee, and the sons of Zebedee, and two others of his disciples.* These last two are not named; some think this is because they were not apostles, while others suggest that they were Philip and Andrew. The seven disciples labored in vain all night long but did not catch a single fish because the divine assistance was lacking; *night* is a fitting symbol for this absence. God permitted this to happen so that the catch of fish that followed would be seen as truly miraculous.

But when the morning was come (which can be understood as the glory of the resurrection), the Lord Jesus appeared to them and *stood on the shore* of the sea.* He appeared on solid ground, not on the water, to show that he was no longer with them on the waves of this corruptible condition but had passed over into an immortal state of life. *Yet the disciples knew not that it was Jesus.* Chrysostom says that Jesus did not show himself immediately so that they would know him by means of the miracle that was about to take place.* Pay careful attention to what is happening here, for it is truly beautiful. He asked them

*John 21:1

*Exp ev
Luke 1.24;
PL 15:1543B

*John 21:2

*John 21:4

*John 21:4

*Hom John
87.2; PG
59:475

if they had any meat to cook and eat, as if he wanted to buy some fish. Spiritually, the food that the Lord asks of us is obedience to the divine commandments, to which we are all obligated, as he had said earlier to his disciples, *"My meat is to do the will of him that sent me."* *They answered him: "No,"* presuming that he was a merchant who wanted to buy fish.

'John 4:34
'John 21:5

When, at his instruction, they had cast their net over the starboard side of the boat, *they were not able to draw it, for the multitude of fishes.* They obeyed, and their obedience bore fruit. These seven fishermen represent preachers in the church. Without Christ's power they are unable to catch anything or accomplish anything; if his interior instruction is lacking, the speaker's tongue labors in vain. It is said that fish avoid nets that are dirty and smelly, nor do they willingly swim into them; those who work with such nets only catch a few small fry or nothing at all. On the other hand, fish are attracted by nets that are clean and fragrant, so the best fish are caught in this way. Christ's net is the Word of God; the fishes, all sinners; the right side, spiritual things; the left, material. The man who preaches for worldly gain or vainglory casts his net over the port side, and his net is foul, so he accomplishes very little; but the preacher who seeks to further the salvation of his hearers with sound doctrine lowers a fragrant net over the starboard side, and he accomplishes a great deal. Nor should this surprise us, since we read in the book of Proverbs, *The Lord knows the ways that are on the right hand, but those are perverse which are on the left hand.*

'John 21:6

'Prov 4:27

When John saw this miracle, which fulfilled what had been said, he recognized Jesus because even the fishes obeyed him, and he *said to Peter: "It is the Lord!"* *Lord* is a title designating power, and Christ had demonstrated his power with the miraculous catch of fishes. According to Bede, he was the first to

'John 21:7

recognize the Lord because of this miraculous catch, or by the sound of his voice, or because he recalled the earlier miraculous catch of fishes.* Peter Cantor writes, "Peter represents the active, laborious aspect of life, while John signifies quiet contemplation. The contemplative points God out to the active. You have been laboring throughout the day; even so, your contemplative side says to you during the night, *'It is the Lord'* so that you will not be so distracted by your labors that you do not attend to him a little."*

Simon Peter, when he heard that it was the Lord, wrapped his robe about him out of respect for Christ, *for he was naked,** that is, he was wearing very little because he was fishing. Bede explains, "It says that Peter was naked by comparison with the amount of clothing he customarily wore. We use the same figure of speech when we see someone scantily dressed: 'Why are you walking around naked?'"* Moved by love and fervent devotion, *he cast himself into the sea*† so that he could come to Jesus more quickly, mindful of the Lord whom he loved so deeply.

But the other disciples came in the ship with great haste *dragging the net with fishes,** because they were not so impetuous as Peter. Impelled by his intense ardor, Peter could not bear to be slowed down by the boat; he jumped into the water and swam to shore to reach the Lord as quickly as possible. In every situation, we find Peter exhibiting greater faith and love than the others. Chrysostom suggests that this incident illustrates perfectly the different gifts of John and Peter: John had more insight, Peter had greater affection, so John was first to recognize the Lord, but Peter first to come to him.* In a spiritual sense, the sea signifies the tribulations of this world. Whoever wishes to come to Christ must plunge into a sea of troubles, because they cannot be avoided; indeed, *through many tribulations we must enter into the kingdom*

*CA John 21:1-11, citing Bede

*Source unknown

*John 21:7

*CA John 21:1-11, citing Bede
†John 21:7

*John 21:8

*Hom John 87.2; PG 59:475

Acts 14:21

of God.* But Christ's servant will pass through these trials secure and unharmed, just as Peter made it safely to shore. The boat carrying the other disciples signifies the church, that is, the sheltering community of believers, as the psalmist says, *"You shall protect*

Ps 30:21

*them in your tabernacle."**

As soon then as they came to land they saw hot coals arranged for cooking lying on the shore, *and a fish laid*

John 21:9

thereon, and bread * nearby. Behold another miracle: Jesus did not increase something he already had, as in the multiplication of the loaves; rather, to further confirm his disciples' faith in the resurrection, he created the burning coals, fish, and bread *ex nihilo* by his divine power. Jesus told them to bring the fish that they had caught at his command. *Simon Peter went up and drew the net to land, full of great fishes, one hundred*

John 21:11

and fifty-three. * Isidore says that all the kinds of fishes in the world can be reduced to this number, and, since the apostles were to fish for all people, this was the

Creat 9.9;
PL 83:937C
John 21:11

exact number they caught.* *And although there were so many, the net was not broken.* * The number and size of the fishes underscores the wonder of this event, both because so many were caught and because the net was not torn.

Calling the disciples to have breakfast, Jesus ate with them, manifesting again the truth of his resurrection by showing them that they were not seeing a ghost or some kind of illusion. They all enjoyed a great feast as he shared that meal with them on the seashore. *And none of them who were at meat dared ask him: "Who are you?"*—not because of fear or dread, but because of their reverence. They also shared a firm conviction, *knowing* with a clear understanding

John 21:12

that it was the Lord, * to whom one must attend with awe and reverence. It would have been pointless to ask this question, and they did not have to ask it: where the truth is obvious, there is no need to ask questions. Chrysostom writes, *"None of them dared ask him*, but with reverent silence and great awe they sat gazing upon him. Somehow *they knew it was the Lord*, but seeing his form so altered, they were stupefied and filled with admiration."* And Augustine teaches, "No one dared to doubt that it was he himself. So great was the evidence that it was Jesus himself who appeared to them that not one of the disciples ventured to doubt, much less deny. In this case, it would have been foolish to inquire."*

Jesus served them with his customary humility: *he took bread and gave it to them,* having blessed it: *and fish in like manner,* and he ate with them. He broke the bread and shared it among them just as he had done before his passion, to affirm his resurrection. Those seven disciples stood reverently and eagerly ate with their Lord. They rejoiced in their hearts as they gazed upon his attractive and joyful countenance. They accepted the tantalizing food from his most sacred hands, and they were refreshed in spirit as well as in body. O, what a banquet that was! Join in their feasting with joyful exultation.

In this spiritual banquet Christ prepares the burning coals of charity that he had carried down to our world, because he had come to cast this fire on the earth and wanted it to be enkindled. He also prepares the bread that refreshes us, which is himself, for he restores us by his teaching and by giving us his own body for food. The Lord also gave his disciples the fish, to show that they must imitate his passion; and he gave bread with the fish, to guarantee that after enduring their sufferings they would experience the joy of being united with him forever. Augustine says,

> The Lord prepared a meal for the seven disciples from the fish he had broiled, together with the fish they had caught, and bread. The roasted fish is the

*Hom John 87.2; PG 59:475

*Tr John ev 123.1; PL 35:1965

*John 21:13

*Piscis assus,
Christus est
passus

Christ who suffered;* he himself is the bread that
came down from heaven. The church is incorporated into this so that she can share in the eternal
blessing, which is why the Lord said, *"Bring the*
*John 21:10
*fishes which you have now caught."** All of us who
cling to this hope, who see in the seven disciples
a figure of all the elect, can realize that we share
in this great sacrament and are united to the same
*Tr John ev
123.2; PL
35:1966
blessedness.*

Pope Gregory explains why the Lord wanted to
share this final meal with his seven fishermen followers:

Why did he choose to share this meal with seven
disciples, unless it were to show that only those
who have been filled with the sevenfold grace of
the Holy Spirit will later partake of the eternal
feast with him? All of our present time unfolded
from seven days, and the number seven often designates perfection. Only those who now overcome
earthly things by the study of perfection, who are
not ensnared by love of this world, who when
beset by temptations of all kinds do not weaken
in their desires—only such as these will dine in
*40 hom 24.6;
PL 76:1187C
the presence of Truth in that final banquet.*

In the earlier miraculous catch of fishes the Lord
signified the church in her present condition; in this
event he signifies her state at the end of the ages,
that is, in the final resurrection of the dead. The sea
symbolizes the present age, while the shore, which
is the limit of the sea, symbolizes the end of the age.
Earlier, Jesus got into the boat because he was with
his disciples on the waves of this passing life; now he
stands on the shore because he has passed over into
the state of life immortal. Earlier, he had not specified
that they should cast their nets to either the right side
*Luke 5:4
or the left: *"Let down your nets for a catch,"** by which
we understand that the net includes both the good
and the bad. Now he says, *"Cast the net on the right*

side of the ship," referring only to those who stand on the right, that is, to the good.

Earlier the size of the catch was not specified: *a very great multitude of fishes*. Now, a specific number of fishes is recorded: *one hundred and fifty-three*. This consists of the number fifty,* signifying the jubilee, when all the people rest from their labors; to this is added the number three, because of the mystery of the Trinity. And we are told that they were large, because all the elect will be great in the heavenly reign, although they will still be of different sizes. Earlier, it was said that the net broke, representing the schisms and heresies that tear the church apart. Now *the net was not broken*, because in that great peace of the saints there will be no divisions. And it was to give greater prominence to this appearance that John inserted, as if it were the conclusion of his account, *"Many other signs also did Jesus in the sight of his disciples, which are not written in this book,"* to serve as a prologue for the narrative that follows.

*Augustine (Tr John ev 122.8) has *ter* ("three times") before *fifty*, omitted by Ludolph

*John 20:30

Christ Questions Peter, Whom He Will Appoint as His Vicar

Attend carefully as well to what follows, for these events are truly beautiful and most useful to us. When that solemn meal was over and all the disciples had been refreshed with the same benefits, *when therefore they had eaten, Jesus said* specifically *to Simon Peter*, because he wished to confer a unique blessing on him, *"Simon, son of John, do you love me more than these,"* that is, more than these others do?" It was as if he were asking, "What will you give me, how will you excel in generosity, because you love me?" According to Alcuin, "In a mystical sense *Simon* signifies *obedient*, and *John*, *grace*. Fittingly Peter is called *Simon, son of John*, that is, *obedient through God's grace*,

*John 21:15

*Com in
John 7.44; PL
100:1001B

to show that, if Peter loved Jesus more ardently than
the other disciples, this was because of God's grace
and not human accomplishment."* The Lord asked
the man who had always and everywhere given him
greater proofs of his affection, *"Simon, son of John, do
you love me more* in truth *than these* others, you, who
have shown greater devotion than they?" The Lord
already knew that Peter not only loved him but loved
him more than the others, but he asked because we
should not only believe in our heart but confess with
our lips.

Peter did not know how much the others loved
Jesus, so he did not presume to say that he loved
him more than they did. He could not see into their
hearts, so he modestly answered without qualifica-
tion, *"Yes, Lord, you know that I love you."*￭ It was as if

*John 21:16

he were saying, "I call you, who plumb the secrets
of the human heart, to be your own witness: I love
you, and because you can see what is hidden, you
know whether I love you more than the others. I do
not know. You know how much I love you, and that I
love you with all my heart; I do not know how much
the others love you." Also, having learned of his own
frailty by his denial, Peter dared not boast about the
degree of his love. He entrusted the judgment of the
degree of his love to Christ, who knows the secrets of
the heart; he would not rely on his self-knowledge,
which had deceived him, but he called on the Lord's
knowledge, saying, *"You know that I love you."* In other
words, "You know better than I do." Humbling himself before the other apostles, he did not say, "I love
you more than they do," but simply, *"I love you,"*
thereby teaching us that we should not vaunt ourselves above others but put others ahead of ourselves.
What he knew about himself, he said: that he loved
the Lord; what he did not know, whether he loved
him more than the others, about that he was silent.

In this he shows us that when we are uncertain about something, we should not feel the need to speak, nor define matters that are unclear to us.

Conferring the pastoral office on Peter, the Lord *said to him: "Feed my lambs."** In other words, "If you love me, prove it by feeding my flock. This is how I will know that you love me, by your caring for my sheep. The example of work is the proof of love." Love of God is shown in love of neighbor; whoever refuses to do a kindness to his neighbor loves God less. Augustine says, "Once Peter had confessed his love, the Lord entrusted his flock to him, as if to say that there was no better way for Peter to show his love for Christ than by being a faithful pastor under the prince of all shepherds."** When Jesus asked a second time if he loved him, and Peter had given the same answer as before, Jesus said again, *"Feed my lambs."** But when the Lord asked a third time if he loved him, *Peter was grieved** to be asked this so often by the one who already knew the answer. He was disturbed because the Lord who knew him also knew all that had not yet happened, and he was afraid that by this repeated questioning Christ wanted to warn him of a future fall, just as he had formerly foretold his threefold denial. He had good reason for concern, and this warning threw him into confusion. According to Chrysostom, Peter feared that he would be chastised again for thinking his love was strong when it was not, as he had been before when he trusted too much in his own strength; so he took refuge in Christ, and he said to him, *"Lord, you know all things*, the mysteries of the human heart, and both the present and the future."** And from the depths of his heart, the lover's voice speaks, *"You know that I love you."** After this third response, the Lord added, *"Feed my sheep."**

Even though Christ was not ignorant of the fervor of Peter's love for him, he asked this question three

*John 21:15

*Sermo 12.1
[147/A]; PL
46:852
*John 21:16
*John 21:17

*Hom John
88.1; PG
59:479
*John 21:17
*John 21:17

times, so that a threefold profession of love could cancel out the triple denial prompted by fear. Augustine writes, "A triple confession is returned for a triple denial so that the tongue may not render less service to love than to fear, and that prospective death may not seem to have prompted more speech than present life." *Ambrose suggests that the Lord did not ask the question in order to learn, but to teach the one whom he would leave behind as his vicar when he had to ascend to heaven.* For the Lord did not want to entrust his lambs and sheep, whom he loved so much that he laid down his life for them, to someone who did not love him; this is why he first asked the shepherd of the church if he loved him, and only then commended to him the care of his lambs and sheep. As it was a sign of fear to deny the shepherd, so it is a sign of love to shepherd the flock.

Chrysostom writes, "'If you love me,' Jesus said, 'lead your brothers and sisters. Show in practice the fervent love you have always professed, and the life you promised to lay down for me, lay down now for my sheep. In this way you will show how highly you value the office of guiding your flock, for this is the greatest sign of love for others.'" * And Gregory: "If, therefore, pastoral care is the sign of love, then the one who does not expend effort to care for the flock is guilty of not loving the chief shepherd."* And Augustine: "For what does *Do you love me? Feed my sheep* mean, except, 'If you love me, do not think to feed yourself, but my sheep—and as *my* sheep, not yours. Seek in them my glory, not yours; my sovereignty, not yours; my gain, not yours.'"* And Bernard:

> It was not for nothing that, in handing over the sheep, he asked three times, *"Simon, do you love me?"* It was, I believe, as though Jesus were saying, "Unless your conscience bears witness that you love me, and love me so ardently and completely—

*Tr John ev 123.5; PL 35:1967

*Exp ev Luke 10.175; PL 15:1848B

*Hom John 88.1; PG 59:479

*Reg Past 1.5; PL 77:19A

*Tr John ev 123.5; PL 35:1967

more than your possessions, your family, and even yourself—that this threefold command of mine will be fulfilled; you must not, on any account, take this charge upon you, nor must you have anything to do with these sheep of mine for whom my blood was shed." Dreadful words indeed, enough to strike terror into the heart of the boldest tyrant! Therefore pay heed, you who have been chosen for this ministry; pay heed, I say, to yourselves and to the precious charge that has been entrusted to you.*

*SC 76.8; PL 183:1154A

Again, Bernard says, "Is it unreasonable to require love of the shepherd who is entrusted with caring for the flock? The man who is so stirred up by the wine of charity that he is inebriated by it—that is the one who should be put in charge of others. He will be forgetful of himself and will seek the things of Jesus Christ rather than his own."*

*De div, Sermo 29.5; PL 183:622C

The first and second times Peter was charged to feed the *lambs*, that is, those who are imperfect and must be fed with milk, while the third time the *sheep* were entrusted to his care, those who are mature and can digest solid food. This is because he was called to be not only a pastor but the pastor of pastors. We find in the church three kinds or grades of the faithful who must be fed like lambs or sheep: the beginners and the proficient, called lambs because they are still growing, and the perfect, who are designated as sheep. Twice he was told, *"Feed my lambs,"* but only once *"Feed my sheep,"* because the weak and the tender have greater need of pastoral solicitude than the strong and the fair-sized, which can fend for themselves and require less attention. Therefore Peter feeds both the lambs and the sheep; he tends both the ewes and the lambs, because he guides both subjects and pastors. He is the shepherd of everyone, because there is no one excluded from the flock that Christ has commended to his pastors.

Consider here the Lord's great goodness and charity. You see clearly how lovingly and diligently he commends our souls to Peter, how he reiterates this commendation and does it yet again. Three times he questions him about love; three times he adds the command *"Feed."* He does not say to Peter, "Shear them, take their milk, slaughter and eat them." No, three times he says, *"Feed:* feed them with the bread of doctrine and sound preaching; feed them with the example of good, honest behavior; feed them with temporal aid." He repeated the command three times to show that those in authority should nourish those under their care with the word of God, good example, and practical assistance.

Peter's Martyrdom Is Foretold

After Peter had responded three times to the Lord that he loved him, and in this way confirmed the special claim of his love, the Lord foretold Peter's martyrdom. It was by this kind of death that Peter would give most evident proof of his love; the church's shepherds should be so full of charity that they are ready to lay down their lives for the flock. Speaking metaphorically, Christ said to Peter,

> *When you were younger* (not in age, but in that vacillation of virtue and resolve which led you to deny me), *you girded yourself and walked where you wished. But when you are old* (not in years, but in that firm conviction you have demonstrated by your confession of love), *you shall stretch forth your hands* to be crucified, for it is in this way that you will be martyred, *and another shall gird you* with ropes to tie you onto the cross, to prolong your agony, *and lead you,*˙ dragging you by main strength *where you do not wish* by natural desire, that is, to death.

˙John 21:18

Instinct and the natural will shrink from death, but the deliberative will can choose, so that an old man by the exercise of his intellectual appetite can be led to the cross because he wants to live with Christ forever. He is following his Master's example, who said, *"Not my will, but yours be done,"* *—even though, if it were possible, Peter would prefer to attain eternal life without the distress of dying. There is a natural bond of love uniting soul and body so that the soul does not wish to be separated from the body, and vice versa. This is why Jesus said, *"where you do not wish,"* that is, according to the instinct of nature, which even one of Peter's age could not but feel. But what is abhorrent to nature can be made attractive by grace, as when the apostle says, *"having a desire to be dissolved and to be with Christ."* *

*Luke 22:42

*Phil 1:23

According to Augustine, whatever the distress of death might be, the power of love can overcome it, love for Christ who freely chose to die for us; if there were little or no distress in the face of death, the glory of the martyrs would not be very great.* Gregory teaches, "Clearly, Peter could not have suffered for Christ had he been unwilling to, but his robust spirit welcomed the martyrdom his weak flesh resisted. He feared the sufferings in his body, but in his spirit he rejoiced in the glory. Even as he shrank from the torments of martyrdom, he willed them. Similarly, we will drink bitter medicine to purge our system when seeking the blessedness of good health; the potion is acrid, but the good health the bitterness restores is desirable."* When the Lord knew that he was loved by Peter, he predicted what the fruit of this love would be, that is, the crown of martyrdom. This is how Peter was destined to feed the flock, bring increase to the church, and follow Christ her Head.

*Tr John ev 123.5; PL 35:1969

*40 hom 3.3; PL 76:1087D

In the Gloss we read, "He who had predicted Peter's denials now foretells his passion. Peter's weakness had prevented him from keeping the promise he had childishly made, but now with manly conviction he is able to suffer for Christ. He no longer feared to forfeit this passing life, because the risen Christ had shown him a new kind of life."*

˙Com John 21:18; PL 114:425A

Chrysostom writes, "Doubtless Peter truly desired to do this, and that is why the Lord revealed to him what was to take place. Peter had said, 'I will lay down my life for you,' and, *'Though I should die with*

˙Matt 26:35

you, I will not deny you,'˙ so the Lord gave him what he wanted. Because Peter was always anxious to experience great danger for the sake of Christ, the Lord said, 'Rely on it, I will give you what you want: the suffering you did not experience in youth you will

˙Hom John 88.1, approx; PG 59:479

have to bear in old age.'"*

Rightly does the text say, *when you are old*, for Peter died fully thirty-seven years after these words were spoken; he certainly was an old man when he suffered. There is a spiritual significance to the fact that Peter endured the agony of the cross when he was elderly and nearing the end of his natural life: after our sins are forgiven, we ought to spend the rest of our lives weeping over them and continue to bear with suffering until death. It says in the Gloss, "Even when sins are forgiven, one must endure the suffering brought on by those sins; the punishment is more drawn out than the fault, lest the sin seem

˙Com John 21:17; PL 114:425A; Aug: Tr John ev 124.5; PL 35:1972

†John 21:19

slight if the punishment ends with it."*

And this he said, signifying by what death, crucifixion, *he should glorify God.*† Peter's martyrdom was ordained for God's glory. He had not been bound along with Christ and led away because he had obscured Christ in the hearts of his hearers by his denial, but by stretching out his arms on the cross like Christ, he later gave glory to him in the presence of his torturers by his constancy in bearing witness to the truth. The death of the saints redounds to Christ's glory because it shows the greatness of the Lord, for they hand themselves over to death for the sake of the truth and faith. The power of love conquers the severe torments of death, so by their death the martyrs certainly glorify God, proclaiming by it how much God should be loved and adored.

And when he had said this, the loving Master sought to lighten the burden by his example and invited Peter to embrace his own manner of death, and *he said to him: "Follow me,"* that is, imitate me," for to follow the Lord is to imitate him. It was as if he had said, "You will be able to endure the terrible agony of the cross to the extent that you remember that by bearing it you are following in my footsteps. Just as I did not shrink from carrying the cross for the sake of your salvation, so you should be mindful that you carry the cross to glorify my name; the palm of martyrdom will be more glorious the more closely you follow in the footsteps of your Master." Earlier Peter had shown a singularly great desire to follow Christ when he said, *"Why cannot I follow you now? I will lay down my life for you."* So here the Lord extracted from him a singular promise, saying, *"Follow me* in the manner of your death. If you love me, *follow me*, come after me; as I laid down my life for you, lay down your life for me. Mount the cross like me; endure the same kind of death I did." He did not say this to Peter by himself, but openly in the presence of the others, because he should be even more willing than the others to lay down his life for his sheep.

"John 21:19

"John 13:37

When he had spoken these final words, the Lord got up and began to walk away from the place where they had eaten. He acted out what he had just expressed verbally to Peter. In the Old Testament, the prophets expressed some things in words and others by gestures; Christ does the same now: having predicted Peter's martyrdom, he began to go, and then said, *"Follow me* in the path that I have foretold to you."

The Question of John's Death

˙John 21:20

˙John 21:20

˙John 21:22

Peter, diverting his eyes from the Lord and *turning about, saw that disciple whom Jesus loved* also *following.*˙ As he was beginning to walk behind Christ, Peter was moved by his love for John to learn how he would die, so he asked, *"Lord, and what shall this man do?"*˙ It was as if he were saying, "Look, I will follow you in your passion. This man, whom I love like my other self—will he die in the same way I do?" It was no business of Peter's what God had in store for John in the future; his concern was simply to obey Christ's word promptly and humbly. Thus, Jesus repeats the simple command: *"Follow me."*˙ Chrysostom comments,

˙John 21:22

˙Hom John 88.2; PG 59:480

> *"So I will have him to remain till I come, what is it to you?"*˙ With these words the Lord instructs us not to be anxious or to investigate a host of topics or to pry into matters about which it is not God's good pleasure to inform us or to scrutinize unnecessary concerns. He said this because Peter and John were motivated by an inopportune compassion, in that they did not want to part from one another. Because they were to be entrusted with the care of the whole world, they could not remain together; their doing so would have been a great loss to the world. For this reason, he said, "I have given you a commission. Attend to it, work at it, struggle with it, accomplish it. If I want him to remain, what is that to you?"˙

˙John 21:23

This saying therefore went abroad among the brethren, that that disciple should not die.˙ They misconstrued our Lord's words to mean that John would still be alive when he returned to judge the world, and they repeated the saying with this interpretation. But had Jesus granted this, it would not have been such a great gift to the disciple, for *to be dissolved and to be with Christ is a thing by far the better.* This interpretation was mistaken; John did die. In order to counter this misunderstanding, the evangelist immediately adds, *And Jesus did not say to him: "He will not die,"* because the sentence of death has been given to all who are born with original sin; *but: "So I will have him to remain* unharmed by persecution *till I come* by summoning him through a natural death to heaven, *what is it to you?"* This question should be interpreted rhetorically: Jesus is not asking, but simply repeating what he had said earlier. John lived to be ninety-nine and preached the Gospel for sixty-eight years.

*Phil 1:23

*John 21:23

This is that disciple who gives testimony of these things that he had heard and seen, which is why his testimony is effective and true, *and has written these things* as a faithful witness, giving an account of them. Because John heard what Jesus said and saw what he did, he could write most fittingly about what happened.

*John 21:24

Putting to one side any comparisons of those two disciples concerning love, we are able to see that in a spiritual sense they symbolize the two ways of life, active and contemplative. By Peter, to whom it was said, *"Follow me,"* the labor of the active life is represented: to this pertains the need to work for the good of others and to bear witness to truth and justice even unto death. John represents the sweetness of the contemplative life: forgetting everyone else, the contemplative clings to God alone, as is signified very well by the words, *"So I will have him to remain till I come,"* meaning, "I want those whom I have intoxicated by tasting me to keep making progress until I return on the Day of Judgment with an eternal reward, when they will move from faith to sight, and from the imperfect contemplation in this world to the perfect contemplation of glory."

The goal of each way is God, and both strive to reach him. The active way loves more than the contemplative, because it feels more the trials of the present life and wants to be freed from them to go to God. But God loves the contemplative way more, because he preserves it longer: it does not come to an end in this world, like the active life, which is why the psalmist says, *"The Lord loves the gates of Sion above all the tabernacles of Jacob."* * This is why the Lord says of the contemplative, *"So I will have him to remain*, that is, wait, *till I come,"* either at the end of the world, or at the contemplative's death, but to the person in the active life he says, *"You follow me."* The contemplative life begins here but does not end here, and it waits until Christ comes to be perfected. The active life is shaped and perfected by the example of Christ's passion, following Christ and suffering for him in this time of probation.

*Ps 86:2

Conclusion

You have certainly seen how many and how wondrous are the things Christ said and did in this appearance. John calls this the third encounter, not according to the number of appearances but according to the days on which Christ appeared. The first appearances took place on the day he rose, when he showed himself to many people; the second appearance was eight days later, when Thomas saw and believed; the third was on this day, when he prepared a meal of fish—but the gospel does not tell us how many days after the octave of Easter this took place. The number three may also refer to the times he appeared to the disciples as a group: the first, when Thomas was absent; the second, when he was present; and the third here at the seashore. In favor of this interpretation is the fact that the evangelist describes them as a group: *to his disciples*. From this time until his ascension, the Lord appeared to his disciples as often as he wished. At last, having given a blessing, he departed from them.

> *Lord Jesus Christ, grant that I, poor as I am, may offer you some little nourishment by obeying your commandments; you are refreshed by our obedience because it gives you great pleasure. Invite me, although I am unworthy, to share in your banquet, so that I may be fed with the broiled fish of the sufferings you endured for us and may bear with my own sufferings for your sake. May I now eat the true bread of your teaching and the sacrament of your body and finally share in the joy of eternal companionship. Grant also, Lord, that I may be found worthy to love you with Peter and bear hardships for your sake, and to be loved by you with John, clinging to you. May I always make progress in this, and persevere to the end. Amen.*

12

Christ Appears in Galilee to the Eleven Apostles and to Five Hundred Disciples

Matt 28:16-20; 1 Cor 15:6

And the eleven disciples went into Galilee in obedience to the words of Christ and the angel, *unto* a specific location on *the mountain where Jesus had appointed them,*· where he had arranged to appear to them. Bede writes, "When the Lord was going to his death, he told his disciples, '*But after I shall be risen again, I will go before you into Galilee.*'· And the angel had told the women, '*And behold he will go before you into Galilee.*'· Thus the disciples went in obedience to the Master's command."· True, the appearance described in the last chapter took place at the Sea of Tiberias, which is in Galilee, but the command did not refer primarily to that event, at which only seven disciples were present, but to another meeting with all of the disciples. Most are of the opinion that this happened on Mount Tabor, at the place where the Lord had been transfigured. There Jesus had foreshadowed the glory of his future resurrection to three disciples, so it was fitting that he revealed the resurrection itself to all the disciples in that same place.

It is thought likely that five hundred followers were also present with the eleven apostles, and that this was the appearance spoken of by Saint Paul: "*Then was he seen by more than five hundred brethren at once.*"· They were not mentioned by Matthew be-

·Matt 28:16

·Mark 14:28
·Matt 28:7

·Chrysostom,
Hom John
88.2; PG
59:480; CA
cites as Bede

·1 Cor 15:6

128

cause the Eleven were Christ's principal followers. Eusebius writes, "Two of the evangelists, Luke and John, relate only the appearances to the Eleven in Judea. The other two sacred authors write that the angel and the Lord himself had instructed not only the Eleven but all the disciples and brethren to hasten to Galilee. This was the meeting Paul referred to when he said, *'Then was he seen by more than five hundred brethren at once.'"* *

*Mar 10; PG
22:1003

How then can we account for the fact that the Acts of the Apostles clearly states that all the disciples were gathered in the Upper Room in Jerusalem, and that there were only one hundred and twenty? Perhaps the disciples who were in Jerusalem with the apostles numbered one hundred and twenty, but there were many other believers scattered among other towns and villages, and the Lord wanted to show himself to all of them together to give them the same consolation the others had received. Rabanus Maurus writes, "The Lord appeared to them on the mountain. This signifies that the body he took from the common clay when he was born like other people is now, in virtue of the resurrection, raised above all earthly things. And by this appearance he admonishes all the faithful: if you want to behold in heaven the full splendor of the resurrection, strive while you are on earth to climb from base cravings to lofty desires." *

*Com Matt
28:16; PL
107:1151C

The Great Commission

And seeing him they adored him and humbled themselves before him, *but some doubted* * because of the novelty of what they beheld. From this it is clear that other disciples were present with the apostles, because the Eleven had received ample proof of the resurrection—even Thomas, who had been more

*Matt 28:17

skeptical than the others. The merciful and gracious Lord strengthens the faith of believers, and he leads the doubtful back to faith by resolving their difficulties and giving them an intimation of the glory that awaits them.

And, to remove any lingering doubts about his resurrection, *Jesus coming, spoke to them, saying: "All power is given to me in heaven and in earth."* * He is speaking here in his human nature, in which he *was made a little lower than the angels,* * not in his divine nature, which he shares equally with the Father. For as regards the divine nature, the Father, the Son, and the Holy Spirit are equal. In his divine nature, Christ exercises sovereignty over all things together with the Father and the Holy Spirit; in his humanity he has received power over everything, and all things have been placed in his hands. He who a little while before had descended from heaven and become man now rules the whole world.

But he has received power not only on earth but also in heaven: exalted in his humanity to the Father's right hand, he has been raised above the angels, and a name has been given him *which is above all names, that in the name of Jesus every knee should bow, of those that are in heaven, on earth, and under the earth.* * Not only is this name more sacred than any other human name, but it is also more holy than all the angels. Never to any creature, human or angelic, was it given to be called Son of God by his very nature, except to him of whom the Father said, *"This is my beloved Son, in whom I am well pleased."* *

Nor was it ever given to any angel or mortal that salvation would be given to the world in his name, but only to God alone, about whom Peter said, *"Neither is there salvation in any other, for there is no other name under heaven given to men, whereby we must be saved."* * In his human nature Christ receives from the

*Matt 28:18

*Heb 2:7

*Phil 2:9-10

*Matt 3:17

*Acts 4:12

Father what in his divine nature he himself gives with the Father. As Severian says, "The Son of God gave to the Son of the Virgin, the God-Man incarnate, the divinity he himself always possessed with the Father." *   ˙Chrysologus, Sermo 80; PL 52:427C

This power, however, is given to him not for him to scorn sinners but to welcome them all without distinction of persons. For this reason, when the Lord instituted the sacrament of baptism he said, *"Going therefore into the whole world, teach the faith to all nations,"* * that is, to every race of people without distinction. From this it is clear that preachers should proclaim the Gospel to everyone, great and small alike. *Going therefore*—this is said to correct the lazy, who do not wish to go; *teach*—this is said to correct the ignorant, who do not know how to teach and yet assume the office of preacher; *all nations*—this is said to correct the selective, who will only seek out certain people.   ˙Matt 28:19

Then he said, *"baptizing them (because unless a man be born again of water and the Holy Spirit, he cannot enter into the kingdom of God)* * in the name* (because of the unity of substance) *of the Father and of the Son and of the Holy Spirit* * (because of the distinction of Persons)." The one gift comes from the one divine nature they share. He did not say, "in the *names* of the Father and of the Son and of the Holy Spirit," but "in the *name*," to show that the indivisible Trinity is one God.   ˙John 3:5   ˙Matt 28:19

And then he directed them, *"Teaching them to observe* by good works and perseverance *all things whatsoever I have commanded you."* * These *things* are the sacraments Christ instituted, other matters pertaining to the catholic faith, and ways of acting established to express love of God and neighbor. The Lord had given his disciples commandments before his passion, but they were to make them known only to the Jews; they were instructed to avoid the Gentiles. This was for a fixed period of time, because the Christian   ˙Matt 28:20

faith was not to be revealed to the whole world before the resurrection.

But after the resurrection he commanded them to go to all nations and, first, to teach them and then to wash them in the sacrament of faith, baptism. Adults should be instructed in the faith before they are baptized; catechesis ought to precede baptism. Immediately after doctrinal instruction and baptism they should be taught how they are to live as true Christians: as James says, we are to be *doers of the word and not hearers only*, and *whoever breaks one of the* •Jas 1:22, 2:10 *commandments violates the whole law.*· This is a reasonable way to proceed: first, learners must be instructed in the faith, and they should not be baptized until they have accepted the faith, because *without faith it* •Heb 11:6 *is impossible to please God.*· Nor does the cleansing of baptism avail them if they do not persevere in good works: *For even as the body without the spirit is dead, so* •Jas 2:26 *also faith without works is dead.*· Therefore it is necessary for us to carry out everything Christ commands.

If this seems to be impossible, let a person simply possess and practice charity. Augustine writes, "Love is a powerful force, brethren. Do you want to see how powerful it is? If some necessity keeps you from doing what God commands, love the one who •En Ps 121.10; commands, and you will fulfill what he commands."· PL 37:1627 He also wrote,

> A person whose heart is full of charity will comprehend the varied abundance and extensive doctrine of the sacred Scriptures without error and safeguard it without effort; as the apostle teaches,
> •Rom 13:10 *"Love therefore is the fulfilling of the law."*· That charity by which we love God and neighbor embraces the whole breadth of the divine pronouncements. The sole heavenly physician teaches us, *"You shall love the Lord your God with your whole heart and with your whole soul and with your whole mind; You*

shall love your neighbor as yourself. On these two commandments depends the whole law and the prophets."*   *Matt
22:37-40

If you lack the leisure to examine the pages
of Scripture in depth, to scrutinize the hidden
meaning of its words and uncover its deepest secrets, then cling to charity, on which God's word
depends. In that way you will hold on to what
you have learned and to what you have not yet
learned: if you know charity, you know the reality on which everything else depends, even the
things you do not know. When you understand
the Scriptures, it is charity that is revealed; charity
lies concealed in what you do not understand. The
person who acts with charity possesses both what
is revealed and what is hidden in God's word.*   *Sermo 350.1;
PL 39:1533

And, "How great love is! If it is lacking, we hold
anything else in vain; if it is present, we have all
things."* And again, "The person who relies on faith,   *Tr John
hope, and charity and keeps a firm hold on these has   ev 9.8; PL
35:1462
no need of the Scriptures, except to instruct others.
Many live in solitude on the strength of these three,
without the Scriptures."*   *De doc
1.39.43; PL
34:36

Charity is so beneficial that it not only supplies
for our defects, but it also makes others' good actions
our own. Pope Gregory says, "The good deeds of
others become ours, even if we cannot imitate them,
when we love them in others, and the good deeds
loved in us belong to those who love them. Let the
envious then consider how great charity is, because
without our effort it makes the good deeds of others
our own."* Augustine concurs: "If you love unity,   *Reg past
then whatever another possesses is yours too. Take   3.10; PL
77:63C
away envy, and what I have is yours and what you
have is mine. Envy divides, charity unites."*   *Tr John
ev 32.8; PL
Through love, a person shares in the merits of all   35:1646
the good works of the church; if charity is lacking, a
person loses the merit of all these good works and of

his own as well. According to Bernard, when love is present even the smallest action is not spurned, and if it is absent even the greatest deed is not accepted.*

*Ps-Bernard, De caritate 3.15; PL 184:591C

To sum up, charity holds pride of place among the virtues: no one can reach the heights of perfection when it is lacking, and one who is full of love has reached perfection.

How Christ Remains Present in His Church

Then, because the Lord had imparted great commands to the disciples, he comforted them and lifted their spirits by saying, *"And behold I am with you all days* by shielding you with divine power and cooperating in your works and labors, and by my presence in the sacrament of the Eucharist, *even to the consummation of the world,* after which, with your labors completed, you will reign with me; as a pledge of which, you have the presence of my divinity and grace with you in the present age." From this it is clear how great a present reward and pledge of future happiness is accorded to the faithful who live devoutly and that the faith will never disappear through all the tribulations of this age.

*Matt 28:20

It was as if he were saying, Chrysostom suggests, "Do not offer excuses, or tell me how difficult my commission is, because *I am with you*, I who make all things easy."* What a great promise, what an invincible shield! *I am with you*: I am fighting through you, I am defending you; fear nothing, go forth securely. *If God be for us, who is against us?* Let us say with the psalmist, *"Through God we shall do mightily: and he shall bring to nothing them that afflict us."**

*Hom Matt 90.2; PG 57/58:789

*Rom 8:31

*Ps 59:14

Chrysostom writes, "Christ did not make this promise only to those who were then present and to those who later joined them; no, he also meant all those who would believe after they were gone, with whom he would remain forever as well. The apostles were not to remain *even to the consummation of the world*, so he was addressing all of the faithful as one body, of which he is the head."* Although the Lord was about to withdraw bodily from the disciples, he would continue to be with them through the presence of his divinity and the influx of spiritual gifts and graces, and he will remain with all the faithful unto the end of the age.

A wise, faithful captain does not leave his ship before it has safely entered port: the church is a ship, and Christ her pilot has not left her, nor will he leave her until she reaches the harbor of heaven. Rabanus Maurus says, "By this it is understood that until the consummation of the world there will never be souls lacking who are worthy to have God dwelling in them."* According to Bede, when Christ says, *"even to the consummation of the world,"* he is expressing the infinite by the finite, for he remains in this present world with his elect, protecting them and guiding them with the hidden promptings of the Holy Spirit; and he will also remain with them after the end, rewarding them and satisfying them forever with his presence.*

Leo the Great teaches, "When he ascended to heaven he did not abandon his adopted children; from there he himself sustains in their combat those whom he invites upward to glory."* He remains with his faithful in the present not only virtually but also by his bodily presence in the sacrament of the Eucharist, in which he is completely present, and at the end of time, they will see him face to face in brilliant light. Chrysostom writes, "Christ tells them he will be with them *even to the consummation of the world* to draw them more strongly to himself, and so that they will not confine their gaze to present realities, which will dissolve with this life, but attend to the future blessings that

*Hom Matt 90.2; PG 57/58:789

*Com Matt 28:20; PL 107:1153B

*CA Matt 28:16-20, citing Bede

*Sermo 72.3; PL 54:392A

last forever. It is as if he were saying, 'The sorrows you endure in this life will disappear with this life, when the consummation of the world occurs; the goods you attain in heaven are eternal.'"*

*Hom Matt 90.2; PG 57/58:790

Conclusion

Consider very carefully these disciples and what was said to them, because they are remarkable events. They stand joyfully around Christ: he shows that he is the Lord of all creation, he commissions them to preach, he gives them the form for baptism, and he imparts to them the utmost strength by saying that he will be with them always. He fills them with a great and indescribable joy, standing in their midst and conversing familiarly with them, *speaking of the kingdom of God.* See what consolation and what tokens of love he gave them! It is clear that they were most anxious to see the Lord, and therefore they deserved to see him. The same is true for us: if we are solicitous and fervent in our desire for the Lord's coming, he will be with us. Those to whom the Lord appeared on the mountain represent contemplatives, because it is said that it was on this mountain that he had been transfigured, and he deigns to show himself frequently to such as these. At length the Lord left them, and, as was his custom, returned to the holy ancestors. The disciples remained for a time, full of joy, and afterward went back to Jerusalem.

*Acts 1:3

> *Lord Jesus Christ, Son of the living God, your appearance on the mountain filled the hearts of your grieving disciples with ineffable joy. Grant to me, a miserable sinner, that as I ascend the mountain of perfection I may labor to trample underfoot worldly desires, and so pass from base pleasures to holy longings. In this way may I be found worthy to behold you on the heavenly summit. Grant me the grace, Lord, to do all that*

*you command. Stay with us, protecting and guiding
us in the present age, and after the consummation of
the world reward us with the feast of your presence
forever. Amen.*

13

Summation of the Resurrection Appearances

Christ appeared on twelve occasions to his disciples between his resurrection and ascension, not counting the two we will consider in connection with the ascension itself; this makes fourteen appearances in all, ten of which are described in the gospels. You can also meditate on others, since it is very likely that the gracious Lord often visited his mother and the disciples, and his beloved follower Mary Magdalen, to comfort and encourage them after the great trial and sorrow of his passion. Augustine seems to be of this opinion about the period after the Lord's resurrection: Not everything, he observes, was written down, but the Lord had frequent encounters with his disciples before he ascended to heaven.* And perhaps he brought with him some of the holy ancestors, especially Abraham and David, to whom a special promise about the Son of God had been made, to behold their most illustrious daughter, his mother, who had found grace before God for them and for everyone and had given birth to the Redeemer. O, with what pleasure they gazed upon her, and how reverently they knelt before her, and how they expressed every blessing within their power, unseen by those who were present with her!

*De cons ev 3.25.84; PL 34:1203

You can also consider here the kindness, love, and humility of the Lord that shines out here as in all his doings: after gloriously conquering and rising from the dead, he chose to linger here for forty days to comfort and strengthen his disciples. It would have

been fitting, after the passage of so many years, after such labors and afflictions, after such an ignominious and bitter death, that the victor should return to his glory and send angels to comfort his apostles and confirm them—but his great love would not permit this. He wanted to meet with them in person and demonstrate the truth of his resurrection *by many proofs,** that is, with evident and sensible signs.   *Acts 1:3
He showed them in his own self the qualities of an immortal body beyond nature, in this way demonstrating the reality of his resurrection and removing any lingering doubts from the apostles' hearts. He showed them his wounds, although such defects are completely alien to the nature of an immortal body; he ate with them and drank with them, although a spiritual body has no need of nourishment. Augustine writes, "The Christian faith does not doubt that after his resurrection the Savior ate and drank with his disciples in his body; his flesh was spiritual, but real. He did so, not because he needed nourishment, but through the power he possessed to do this."*   *De civ Dei 22.19.2; PL 41:781

Apart from these proofs, Luke mentions others in his Acts of the Apostles. Evidence for the truth of the resurrection is that *for forty days* he appeared to them in various ways, *speaking of the kingdom of God.** This   *Acts 1:3
should not be understood to mean that he appeared to them each and every day, showing himself to their eyes, allowing them to touch him, and eating and drinking with them, as he had been accustomed to formerly. It would not have been proper to be with them continually as he had been before, lest they think that he had simply returned to mortal life. He appeared to the disciples at intervals and did not abide with them continually to show that he had risen to life immortal, distinguished from human life here.

Christ did not ascend immediately after his resurrection for several reasons: to demonstrate his resurrection in many ways, to refresh the disciples with his consolations, and to give us an example of patience, so that we would await our reward with equanimity. He had been dead for forty hours: four hours on the evening of Good Friday, and the thirty-six hours of two nights and a day. But he spent forty days with his disciples after his resurrection, because divine comfort exceeds human sorrow. He did this for them, and also for us—but we give it no thought. He loved passionately, and he still so loves, but he is not loved in return, even though we should not only be warmed by such love but set ablaze by it.

We read that after his resurrection the Savior did not appear to wicked or worldly people, but only to his apostles and other faithful disciples. It was not fitting for Jesus, having risen from the dead immortal and eternal, to show himself to those who were dead to God and separated from life, which is Christ. He himself had said earlier, *"Yet a little while and the world,* that is, those who look only with the eyes of flesh, *sees me no more. But you see me."** Theophylact writes, "Henceforth he does not keep company with other people, because after the resurrection his conversation is worthy of divine realities, not human ones. This is also a model for our future resurrection, in which we shall be companions of the angels and the children of God."*

*John 14:19

*Exp Acta 1:3, approx.; PG 125:506

He showed himself to his faithful disciples so that the living one should be seen by the living. As Augustine notes, when the Lord rose he was only seen by his own.* In the Acts of the Apostles, Peter says, *"Him God raised up the third day and gave him to be made manifest, not to all the people, but to witnesses preordained by God, to us, who ate and drank with him, after he arose again from the dead."** It was appropriate that he did not appear to everyone, but to *witnesses preordained*: the lowest things are raised up to the

*Sermo 265.2; PL 38:1220

*Acts 10:40-41

highest through some intermediaries, so he chose certain mediators through whom the resurrection could be revealed to the whole world. Thus the Lord appeared over the course of forty days to his disciples in many ways, approaching them and speaking with them. His words provide instruction for our faith, his promises nurture our hope, and his heavenly gifts enkindle our charity. And, according to Jerome, he revealed immortality to mortals so that we might be grateful when we understand what we have been and know what we will be in the future.˙

˙Cumm
Mark 16:7;
PL 30:641D

Concerning the spiritual meaning of the afore-mentioned appearances and the two that follow, Bede writes,

> By the frequent appearances in his risen body the Lord wants to show that he is present by his divinity everywhere to the desires of those who are good. He appeared at the tomb to the women who were mourning; he is present to us when we are profitably saddened by his absence. He hastened to meet those who were returning from the tomb, so that they could proclaim the resurrection about which they had learned; he is present to us when we rejoice to share faithfully with our neighbors the good things we know. He appeared at the breaking of the bread to those who thought he was a stranger and invited him to dine with them, he is present to us when we freely bestow on strangers and the poor whatever goods we can, and he is present to us in the breaking of the bread, when we partake of the bread and wine that are the sacrament of his Body and Blood with a pure and chaste conscience.
>
> He appeared in secret to those who were speaking about his resurrection; he is present to us when, by his gift, we do the same; he is always present to us when we take time from exterior labors and come together to talk about his grace.

He appeared to them when they were hiding behind locked doors for fear of the Jews, and he appeared when their fear abated somewhat and they openly sought him out on the summit of the mountain. . . .[1] He appeared to those who were fishing and by his appearance aided them with divine blessings; he is present to us when we carry out our responsibilities with an upright intention, and with his benevolent assistance he aids our just labors. He appeared to those who were reclining at table; he is present to us when, according to the admonition of the apostle, *"whether you eat or drink, or whatsoever else you do, do all to the glory of God."* *

*1 Cor 10:31

He appeared first in Judea, then in Galilee, and then in Judea again on the day he ascended to heaven; he was present to his church when she was limited to the confines of Judea; he is present to her now when, having left the Jews because of their unbelief, she has crossed over to the Gentiles; and he will be present in the future when he returns to Judea before the end of the world, and, as the apostle says, once the multitude of nations has come in, *so all Israel should be saved.* *

*Rom 11:26

Last, he appeared to them as he was ascending into heaven; he will also be present to us after death so that we will be worthy to follow him to heaven, if before death we have taken care to follow him to the place from which he ascended, Bethany, which means *house of obedience*. Indeed, he came to Bethany when he himself was about to ascend because, as the apostle says, *"He became obedient unto death, even to the death of the cross. For which cause, God also has exalted him."* * We will come to the same place if we do what he has told us and direct ourselves to what he has promised: *"Be faithful unto death, and I will give you the crown*

*Phil 2:8-9

---

[1] Ellipses here and below indicate the translator's abbreviation of Ludolph's lengthy quotation from Bede.

of life." And so it happens that he remains with us to the end of life by the bestowal of his grace, and he will raise us up after this life to behold with him the reward of heavenly life.*

*Rev 2:10

*Hom 3
[2.8]; PL
94:148B–149B

As with the forty days of Lent, so Christ also sanctified the fifty days of Eastertide for us, and in a mystical way he instituted both solemn seasons. Bede says,

It was the divine authority of our Lord and Savior himself, and not any merely human authority, that first prescribed these solemn seasons of forty days and fifty days for us. He instituted the Lenten season by his fast of forty days and forty nights in the desert. When he had overcome the wiles of the tempter, he delighted in the ministrations of angels. In this he gave us an example: we must evade the deceits of our spiritual adversaries through the chastisement of the flesh and so be welcomed into the company of the angels. He also directed us to celebrate the fifty days of paschal joy, because after his resurrection *he showed himself alive after his passion, by many proofs, for forty days appearing to them,* and by his frequent visits to them made this a season of great rejoicing.

*Acts 1:3

Nor should we think of this simply as a foretaste of the joy we will have with him in the world to come but as a true and ineffable manifestation of his mercy for us now. Although he had left behind the weakness of mortal flesh, which had been transformed into glory by the resurrection, he still deigned to associate with his disciples. He did this so that he could have them as his companions in heaven, and by his familiarity with them he could engrave more deeply into their hearts the commandments that lead to the kingdom of God and could strengthen them by reminding them of what he had promised before his passion: *"And I allot to you, as my Father has allotted to me, a kingdom; that you may eat and drink at my table, in my kingdom."*

*Luke
22:29-30

When he ascended into heaven he did not take
from them the delight of his earlier presence;
rather, he increased it by the promised anointing
of the Holy Spirit. At length they *went back into
Jerusalem with great joy, and they were always in the
temple, praising and blessing God.* They taught us
that we, too, should prolong the joy of this solemnity with happiness, praises, and blessings
like those with which they awaited the coming
of the Holy Spirit, up to that fiftieth day, which
the Greeks call *Pentecost.* Rightly, then, during
this solemn season we enjoy festive meals and
sing heavenly anthems: out of reverence for the
Lord's resurrection, in memory of the Lord's eating with his disciples, and because of our hope for
future rest and immortal life. . . . Rightly, then,
do we observe forty days' fast, to remind us that
we must struggle throughout this earthly life in
order to attain life eternal. We also fittingly honor
our future state of blessedness under the image of
fifty days by mitigating our fasts, singing *Alleluia,*
and standing for prayer: these are fitting presages
of the perpetual rest and praise that will mark our
resurrection.

*Acts
24:52-53

*Hom 10
[2.16]; PL
94:186B–187D

*Lord Jesus Christ, after gloriously rising from the dead
you appeared, living and immortal, to your faithful disciples. For forty days you graciously lingered in their
company and spoke tenderly with them, and by many
convincing arguments you discoursed with them about
the reign of God. You consoled them and ate with them
to remove every shadow of doubt from their hearts, so
that they would be convinced and believe that you were
truly risen. Good and loving Jesus, I pray that I may
be counted among those witnesses chosen by God to
testify to your resurrection, not only by my words, but
above all in deed and in truth. Amen.*

14

The Ascension

Mark 16:14-20; Luke 24:48-53; Acts 1:4-14

We should attend carefully to the Lord's ascension, for it is a truly solemn event. Let eager attention expand our souls: the Lord is completing the course of his earthly pilgrimage and is withdrawing from us bodily, so his final words and actions merit special study. Put everything else out of mind and give total, devout, and humble attention to what the bridegroom, your Lord and God, says and does as he prepares to leave.

The *Lord Jesus knowing that his hour was come, that he should pass out of this world to the Father, having loved his own who were in the world, he now loved them unto the end.*[*] He came to his eleven apostles, who were staying with Mary and other disciples on Mount Sion. They were all residing in that neighborhood: the mother of Jesus and the Eleven dwelt in the Upper Room where the Lord had celebrated the Last Supper, and the other followers were dispersed in nearby homes. When the apostles and the Blessed Virgin (and perhaps other leading members of the community) were resting or eating in that room, the Lord appeared to them; the loving Master ate with them before his departure, as a token and memorial of his joy and his special love for them. Since the apostles would see him no more in the flesh, he dined with them one final time, as friends eat and drink together before they part from one another. They all shared most joyfully in this last meal at the third hour with

*[*] John 13:1

145

the Lord, so that they could all bear witness and describe what they had together seen and heard.

The Lord Jesus knew that the time had come for him to return to the one who had sent him, so *he upbraided them with their* former *incredulity*, which gave place to belief, *and hardness of heart*, so that by being filled with charity their hearts of stone would become hearts of flesh, *because they did not believe them* ·Mark 16:14 *who had seen him after he was risen again* from the dead. They themselves had not believed until they saw him, but the Gentiles would believe the Gospel they proclaimed after the resurrection without seeing the risen Christ. The Lord chided the disciples all the more because they were soon going to preach the Gospel to all the nations. It was as if he gave them to understand, "Heralds of the resurrection, how much more you should have believed before you saw me than the Gentiles who will believe your proclamation of the Good News even though they will not see me." After this reprimand, he told them that they were to go into the world to preach. He also corrected them like this before leaving them so that the awareness of their failings would keep them humble. On the verge of departing, he brought home how pleasing the virtue of humility was to him, as if he wanted to recommend it particularly to their attention. His parting words were to lodge deep in the hearts of his hearers and remain there.

The Lord Gives the Great Commission

Having admonished them with these words, *he said to them,* "Making constant progress, *Go into the whole world,* not just Judea, *and preach the gospel* that excels all other doctrines." And Christ said further, ·Mark 16:15 *"Preach the gospel to every creature."* This can mean to every human being without exception, that is, to all humanity, for whose sake everything else was created. Or it can mean that all of creation is represented in us, because we have a commonality with the rest of creation. We exist, like inanimate objects; we have life, like vegetation and plants; we have feeling, like animals; we have understanding, like angels; and so *every creature* refers to humanity. What Jesus commands here, however, was not to be done until they had received the Holy Spirit and been confirmed in their mission; before that, at Christ's instruction, they were not to leave Jerusalem. Christ had formerly said, *"Go not into the way of the Gentiles."** But now he says, *"Preach the gospel to every creature,"* that is, to all nations, first to the Jews and then to the Gentiles, because God *will have all men to be saved and to come to the knowledge of the truth.** `*Matt 10:5`

`*1 Tim 2:4`

Jesus then added, promising salvation to those who believe and warning of condemnation to those who do not, *"He that believes and is baptized shall be saved, but he that does not believe shall be condemned."** In other words, *he that believes* with a faith shaped through love *and is baptized shall be saved* by eternal deliverance from his sins and the punishment they deserve. *He that does not believe shall be condemned* justly to eternal damnation because of his lack of faith. Jesus did not say, "He that is not baptized shall be condemned," because faith without baptism can save a person—provided the person is prevented from receiving baptism from circumstance and not from contempt for religion. Nor should anyone presume on a faith that does not express itself in action, because such faith is powerless to save. *Faith without works is dead,** as are works without faith. Pope Gregory writes: "Perhaps each of us may say to himself, 'I have believed; I will be saved.' What we say is true, if we support our faith with works. The faith is genuine when our deeds do not contradict our words; `*Mark 16:16`

`*Jas 2:26`

we believe with profit if we put into practice what
we profess."*

*40 hom 29.3;
PL 76:1214D

Jesus went on to promise signs that would be given
to confirm and augment their faith: *These signs shall follow them that believe* on account of their faith, signs that
will be given at the opportune time according to need:
In my name invoked with honor, that is, in the power
of my name, *they shall cast out devils*; we read many
accounts of unclean spirits obeying the apostles. *They
shall speak with new tongues*; this the apostles and other
believers did at Pentecost. *They shall take up serpents*
without being harmed; we read of this happening to
Paul. *And if they drink any deadly thing, it shall not hurt
them*; this occurred to John the evangelist. *They shall
lay their hand upon the sick, and they shall recover;* many
believers performed such signs.

*Mark
16:17-18

We read that in the primitive church these won-
ders were done not only by the apostles and leading
members of the community but also by many ordinary Christians. These signs were given to convert unbelievers and to strengthen the nascent faith by means
of such miracles. If someone asks why preachers and
the faithful today do not perform such signs, Gregory
answers that the catholic faith has been proved suffi-
ciently by the miracles of Christ and his apostles, so
it is not necessary to repeat such proofs now; a tree is
watered frequently when it is first planted, but once
it takes root that is no longer required.* In subsequent
ages also God has performed many miracles, as is
evident during the age of martyrs and confessors.

*40 hom 29.4;
PL 76:1215BC

According to Gregory, God continues to do spiritually in the church what he did physically in former
times. When priests exorcise people, baptize them,
and call them to repentance, *they cast out devils*; when
believers give up worldly talk and speak of the mysteries of faith and the new law, *they speak with new
tongues*. When they drain the venom of malice from

the hearts of others by good words of exhortation, *they take up serpents.* When they hear dangerous advice but are not led to commit evil deeds, *they drink any deadly thing and it does not hurt them.* When they see a neighbor faltering in belief or good works and give encouragement by their own positive example, or by their prayer heal those who are spiritually ill and reconcile them to God, *they lay their hand upon the sick, and they recover.*

*40 hom 29.4; PL 76:1215C–1216A

These miracles are all the greater because they are spiritual, and it is not bodies but souls that are affected. We also learn from this that our words must be confirmed by deeds. Again, *they cast out devils* who repel the assaults of the devil by faith and the sign of the cross; *they speak with new tongues* who avoid idle chatter and proclaim God's praises; *they take up serpents* who effectually restrain detractors; *they drink any deadly thing and it does not hurt them* who turn a deaf ear to wicked suggestions or cruel attacks; *they lay their hand upon the sick and they recover* who by good words and actions bring others back from sin and confirm them in good things. These and similar spiritual signs are better than physical ones, inasmuch as the soul is superior to the body.

The Promise of the Holy Spirit

Then Jesus told them, "*And you* especially *are witnesses of these things* that you have seen and heard, what I have said and done in your midst." And, lest they be thrown into confusion, thinking, "How can we unlettered men bear witness to the Jews and Gentiles who killed you?" he added, "*I send the promise of my Father upon you* to help you, that is, the Holy Spirit, in a visible manner so that you will be able to bear witness and preach the truth of the Gospel unwaveringly everywhere."

*Luke 24:48

*Luke 24:49

So that they would not presume to preach until they were ready, he added, *"But stay in the city* of Jerusalem *till you be endued* completely with spiritual armor, *with* that *power from on high*˙ that is heavenly and not earthly, the grace of the Holy Spirit." The same instruction is recorded in the Acts of the Apostles: *And eating together with them, he commanded them that they should not depart from Jerusalem, but should wait for the promise of the Father.*˙ Chrysostom says,

˙Luke 24:49

˙Acts 1:4

> Just as no one would launch an invasion until his soldiers were well armed, so Christ would not allow his disciples to go into battle before the Holy Spirit had descended upon them. But why did the Spirit not come while Christ was still present, or immediately after his departure? Because it was fitting for them first to desire grace, and only then to receive it. We are most aware of God when difficulties press upon us. He said, *"till you be endued with power from on high"* but did not say when this would happen, so that they would be constantly watchful. Why marvel that he does not reveal our last day to us, when he would not even make known this day that was close at hand?˙

˙Hom Acta
1.4, 5; PG
60:19, 20

Even though Christ had imparted an understanding of the Scriptures to his disciples and commissioned them to preach, he postponed the execution of this office until they had received the Holy Spirit through a visible sign; this suggests that before someone begins to preach, he should possess both sufficient knowledge of Scripture and the grace of the Holy Spirit. Gregory cautions,

> It should be noted that there are people barred from preaching by immaturity or lack of preparation, but an unseemly haste impels them to preach anyway. They should be warned that by arrogating this onerous task to themselves they may subsequently lose for themselves the way to a better

life. Let them learn a lesson from Truth himself,
who could have prepared his disciples instantly
had he chosen to, but who gave an example to
his followers, lest those who were unprepared
should dare to begin preaching. After having
fully instructed his disciples about the virtue of
preaching, he immediately added, *"But stay in
the city till you are endued with power from on high."*
We will stay in the city if we confine ourselves to
the cloister of our own minds and do not wander
about outside by idle chatter, so that we can be
endued perfectly with divine power. Then we can
as it were come out of ourselves to instruct others.* *Reg past 25;
PL 77:98AB

The Disciples Are Led Out
to the Mount of Olives

When they had all eaten, *he led them out as far as
Bethany,** because that village was on the slope of the *Luke 24:50
Mount of Olives, which was their destination. *He led
them out* so that they could witness his ascension,
which suggests that the noisy city does not lend itself to the contemplation of divine things. First, *he
led them out* of the city, to show that we have here
no abiding city; then he led them to *Bethany*, which
means *house of obedience*.[1] Christ had descended by
obedience and humbled himself even unto death, and
because of this obedience he deserved to ascend and
be exalted in heaven. As we read: *He humbled himself, becoming obedient unto death, for which cause God
also has exalted him,** so that he might brand with the *Phil 2:8-9
works of obedience those who were to cross over to
heavenly joys. Heaven can only be won as a reward
for obedience: just as disobedience caused humanity's expulsion from Paradise, so obedience brings us

---

[1] Jerome translates *Bethany* as *house of affliction* or *house of obedience* (Int nom; PL 23:839).

back. Also, according to Bede, *he led them out as far as Bethany* because that village was located on the side of the Mount of Olives and thus symbolizes that the *house of obedience* (the church of faith, hope, and love) is founded in the side of that high mountain, Christ.*

*Com Luke 24:50; PL 92:633B

Having led them out of the city, Jesus told them to go to the Mount of Olives: there they would see him ascend to heaven, because that was the place he had chosen for his departure. Then he vanished from their sight. The mountain signifies the heights the soul attains in contemplation, and the olives represent the abundant sweetness attained by devotion; once these have been experienced, there remains only the ascent to heaven itself. The eleven apostles, in company with the mother of the Lord and the other disciples, men and women alike, immediately climbed the Mount of Olives, where the Lord appeared to them again. Thus we understand that there were two appearances on this day. Watch each of the disciples carefully now and see what they are doing.

*Acts 1:6

Then some *who were come together asked him:* "Lord, will you at this time restore again the kingdom of Israel?"* Ignorant of anything save worldly wisdom, these men saw that foreigners ruled over them and that the Jews were subject to a Roman governor; they wanted sovereignty restored to the Jewish nation and an earthly kingdom established. They believed that the Lord, as king of the Jews, would now bring about this restoration and free them from foreign domination. This is what the two disciples on the road had thought: *"But we hoped that it was he that would redeem Israel."** Others, better informed, knew that such a restoration would not occur until the Final Judgment, and they were inquiring whether the kingdom of Israel was now to be restored spiritually by the release and spread of the church. Augustine writes,

*Luke 24:21

Therefore Christ's disciples, gathering from his appearance that he was about to ascend, inquired of him, "If you are manifesting yourself at this time, when will the kingdom of Israel come?" What kingdom? The kingdom of which we say, "Thy kingdom come," the kingdom where those who will be placed at his right hand will hear, *"Come, you blessed of my Father, possess the kingdom prepared for you from the foundation of the world."* * But when will this kingdom come, the kingdom of Christ's own, when the proud are deposed and humble raised up? What does it matter to you when it will come? Live as though it is coming today, and you need not fear its coming.*

*Matt 25:34

*Sermo 265.2;
PL 38:1220

The Lord did not give a precise answer to their question, but his response suggests that such a restoration will be delayed for a long time. *He said to them: "It is not for you to know the time or moments, which the Father has put in his own power."* * In effect, Jesus says to them, "Do not inquire about matters that are secret or are beyond your ken. Rather, be concerned with what will happen to you, for in truth *you shall receive the power of the Holy Spirit coming upon* you to purify and strengthen you so that you can proclaim my word and bear witness to my teaching, *and you shall be witnesses of me* and my actions, doctrine, death, and resurrection, first *in Jerusalem, and* then *in all Judea, and Samaria, and* finally *even to the uttermost part of the earth."* * It is as if he were tacitly saying that before the restoration they spoke of, the news of the Gospel would spread not only throughout Jerusalem but also to the limits of Judea and Samaria and throughout the whole world. Augustine asks,

*Acts 1:7

*Acts 1:8

How can we think that this commission given to the apostles has been fulfilled, when even now there are peoples who are just beginning to hear

the good news, and it has not yet reached some
nations at all? Certainly the Lord did not give this
commission only to the apostles, as if they alone
could fulfill such a responsibility to preach. Similarly, the words of the Lord, *"I am with you all
days, even to the consummation of the world,"* were
spoken only to them, but in fact this promise was
given to the whole church, whose members are
born and die down through ages until the future
consummation of the world.*

*Matt 28:20;
Ep 199.49; PL
33:923
*Acts 1:9

And when he had said these things to comfort them,
he embraced each of them warmly, because, according to Ambrose, he gave each apostle a kiss of peace.*
Then, saying farewell, *and lifting up his hands* to the
Father, *he blessed them,* that is, wished, promised, and
conferred on them all good things to protect them
from the enemy and increase their heavenly blessings. It may also be, as Theophylact suggests, that by
this blessing he bestowed strength to sustain them
until the coming of the Holy Spirit.* At his departure,
Christ blessed his disciples as a father does when he
leaves his children, and he did this for two reasons.
First, they needed a blessing: Jesus had prayed earlier, *"While I was with them, I kept them in your name,"*
and he now asked that they be protected from evil
after he was gone. Second, he blessed them to show
that his love for them continued to the very last moment; *having loved his own who were in the world, he
loved them unto the end.*

*Source
unknown
*Luke 24:50

*En ev Luke
24:36-44; PG
123:1126B

*John 17:12

*John 13:1

The Ascension

Having finished these things, Christ by his own
unaided power ascended *while they looked on.* This
was seen by those deemed worthy of this privilege;
they followed him with their eyes, yearning to go
with him. Borne by his own power, he triumphantly

*Acts 1:9

entered into the highest heavens, from which he
had come. Then his mother and the others who
were watching him ascend prostrated themselves
on the ground in adoration; they could not refrain
from weeping at Christ's departure, but their joy
was greater as they watched him gloriously rising
to heaven. O, how gladly the mother would have
left this world with her son! But the Lord wished
her to remain behind for a time to help confirm the
disciples' faith. Anselm writes this:

> But, O good Jesus, how could you bear to enter
> into your glorious reign while leaving your most
> loving and devoted mother as one bereaved amid
> the miseries of this world and not raise her up
> immediately to her throne? It seems to me that
> it was necessary for our faith that she remain in
> the company of his apostles for a time. True, they
> were instructed in all truth by the Holy Spirit; but
> by the same Spirit she enjoyed an incomparably
> profound and clear understanding of that same
> truth. Many aspects of the truth were revealed
> through her, because she knew many of the mys-
> teries of our Lord Jesus Christ not only by un-
> derstanding but also from firsthand experience.
>
> Nor could the delay of Mary's assumption in
> any way dampen her immense love and joy; she
> had received such an abundance of these that they
> only increased when she knew that she was where
> God, whom she loved more than others, wanted
> her to be. So, wherever Mary found herself she
> rejoiced that she was in God and God was in her.
> Her greatest joy came from knowing that wher-
> ever she was and whatever she did, this was what
> was most pleasing to God's wisdom.*

*Eadmer,
De exc 7; PL
159:571A–D

Let us note in passing that Christ did four things:
he led his disciples out of the city, he brought them to
Bethany, he blessed them, and he ascended. We can
interpret this to mean that Christ first leads sinners

away from sin, then he brings them to Bethany, *the house of obedience*, and there changes their status; next he blesses them, filling them with grace; and finally he ascends, that is, he enables them to rise to higher things, so that *they shall go from virtue to virtue.*˙

˙Ps 83:8

As he ascended, the Lord Jesus brought with him that noble throng, the ancestors held captive in the infernal regions who had been liberated at his resurrection. The gates of heaven swung open, and, as the prophet Micah had foretold, the exiles followed their leader into God's kingdom.˙ They became fellow citizens with the angels and members of the household of God; places left vacant by the fallen angels were filled, the Eternal Father's honor was increased, Christ's own triumph was manifest, and his position as the Lord of Hosts was confirmed. The Lord—glorious, shining, ruddy, splendid, and joyful—went before them to show the way, and they followed him singing and rejoicing.

˙Mic 2:13

Michael the Archangel had gone ahead, entering the heavenly homeland to announce that the Lord was ascending there. At this word all the blessed spirits hastened to meet him, falling into formation in their varied choirs. Not a single one lagged behind; all went to meet their Lord. Bowing down with all the reverence they could, they escorted him, singing ineffable canticles and songs. Who could set forth their hymns and songs or describe their joy? Or who could do justice to the joyful scene of the blessed spirits and our holy ancestors rushing into one another's arms? All were rejoicing and singing psalms; as the prophet said, *"God is ascended with jubilee."*˙ The second half of the verse in the psalm, *"and the Lord with the sound of trumpet,"* refers to preaching of the apostles, who had just been commanded by the Lord, *"Go into the whole world and preach the gospel to every creature."*˙ Only after receiving the Holy Spirit has *their sound gone forth into all the earth.*˙

˙Ps 46:6

˙Mark 16:15
˙Ps 18:5

The Lord ascended very slowly and distinctly to console his mother and the other disciples who could see him. Then *a bright, shining cloud received him out of their bodily sight,* because the brilliance of the cloud prevented them from seeing him anymore. Those who had known Christ according to the flesh would no longer know him in that way. Until he reached the clouds, his body had the same form it had had before the passion, but when he was taken into the cloud, his body appeared as it had done on the mountain. Christ was surrounded by a mandorla-shaped cloud, but it was not a vehicle to carry him; he required no help from a cloud or from angels, because he was borne up by his own power.

Christ's mother, Mary Magdalen, the disciples, and the others stood intently watching the sky as long as they could see him. Ambrose writes, "The blessed apostles stood in a state of suspense watching the Lord ascend, following him with their eyes because they could not follow him bodily. Even though he disappeared from their human sight, he was not lost to the eyes of faith: they followed Christ to the cloud with their eyes, but they accompanied him into the heavens by faith's devotion. Knowing that our faith is in heaven with the Lord, the apostle said, *'But our conversation is in heaven.'"* *

*Acts 1:9

*Phil 3:20;
Maximus of
Turin, Hom
61 [44]; PL
57:373A

The Angels Appear

And while they were beholding him going up to heaven out of their sight, behold two angels in the form of *men stood by them in white garments,* so that their vesture reflected their great joy. *They said: "Men of Galilee, why do you stand here looking up to heaven?"* * It was as if they were saying, "You are standing here gazing at the sky as if you are oblivious of what you should do. Return to the city and await the promise of the

*Acts 1:10-11

Father, as he instructed you. Go back, but do not expect Jesus to return now the way he left; rather, at the end of time he *shall come as you have seen him going* *Acts 1:11 *into heaven."* Augustine says, *"He shall come as you have seen him going into heaven,* that is, he will judge in the human form in which he was judged, so that the prophecy may be fulfilled: *They shall look upon* *Zech 12:10; *him whom they have pierced."* And again, "Because Tr John ev we believe he will return, let us await him in such a 36.12; PL way that his coming does not catch us off guard, as 35:1670 punishment does with the guilty now. Present punishment is an image of what the future holds. Let us beware: if we are not corrected by present blows, we *Ps-Aug will be severely condemned in the future."*

*Ps-Aug
Sermo
41.5–6;
Caillau Aug
Supp 1, 61

The Disciples Return to Jerusalem

Pause here to reflect on the great kindness of the Lord Jesus: as soon as he disappeared from their sight he dispatched his angels to them. He did this to comfort them as they mourned his absence and so they would not linger there, tiring themselves out standing on that spot, but would return to Jerusalem to await the promise of the Father. When the angels disappeared, the disciples knelt to adore Christ, the *Ps 131:7 God-Man, *in the place where his feet* last *stood.* Then *they returned to Jerusalem from the mount that is called Olivet* on account of the many olive trees there, *which* *Acts 1:12 *is near Jerusalem, within a sabbath day's journey.*

Jesus at the Father's Right Hand

Opening the gates of Paradise, hitherto closed to the human race, the Lord Jesus entered in joy and triumph surrounded by the rejoicing multitude. Augustine observes that after his ascension, Christ sits at the right hand of the Father, but that this language should not be taken literally, as if the human Christ sat on the right and the Father sat on the left. Rather, he is said to sit because he has received from his Father the authority to judge; he sits in judgment.* *De fide 7.14; PL 40:188

To sit at the right can be said of Christ by virtue of his divinity: this sitting denotes equality with the Father, because he reigns together with the Father in equality of majesty in the divine nature that he shares with the Father. If sitting at the right is considered in terms of Christ's humanity, it can be understood in two ways. First, his human nature is united to his Godhead, and this sitting suggests an association of honor: his humanity is given the same worship accorded to his divinity because it is united to the Word, who is God; in this sense to say that Jesus sits at the right hand means that Christ's humanity rests in the glory of his divinity.

Second, the right hand suggests the more honored place. It is deservedly said of Christ that he sits at the right hand of God: he sits, because he has labored; he sits at the right hand, because for long he labored in sinister adversity; he sits at the right hand of God, because exaltation follows upon humiliation. Christ is said to sit because he is equal to the Father in his authority to judge. But he is also said to stand because he assists his soldiers in their present conflict. Stephen beheld *Jesus standing on the right hand of God** because *Acts 7:55 Christ was his defender and champion in his tribulation. Sitting designates rest and judgment; standing symbolizes helping and fighting. Therefore, Christ seated at the Father's right hand appears continually before his most gentle face, showing him the wounds he received for our sake *to make intercession for us.** *Heb 7:25

Rejoicing in Heaven and on Earth

All the holy ancestors and blessed spirits sang jubilant hymns before God. If Moses and the children of Israel sang a hymn to God after they crossed the Red Sea, and Moses' sister—the prophet Miriam—and the other women following her beat drums and sang choruses, how much more did this throng, freed from all adversity, make joyful music? Everyone in that holy place sang psalms and hymns, everyone rejoiced, everyone exulted, everyone shouted and clapped their hands, everyone danced and shared their delight. Truly now was heard throughout the heavenly Jerusalem a song of joy, and the cry of *Alleluia!* from the lips of all echoed through every street. Never since the creation of the world had there been such a feast, such a solemn Pasch, celebrated in that homeland; nor will the like ever be seen again, except perhaps after the Day of Judgment, when all the elect in heaven receive their glorified bodies.

Accordingly, truly great and solemn is this feast. Everything that God had done before was done to reach this day. The heavens and the earth and all they contain were made for our sake, but we were made to possess heavenly glory, a glory none could attain after the Fall, regardless of how righteous they were. But everything reached its completion on this great and wondrous Ascension Day. This is truly the most solemn feast for our Lord Jesus, who today began to reign at the Father's right hand and take his rest after his laborious pilgrimage. It is also a true celebration for the angelic spirits. They welcome their Lord with fresh joy, and they witness today in the multitude of the blessed the beginning of their own restoration: their numbers, diminished by sin, are now renewed by the Lord Jesus. If *there shall be joy before the angels of* *Luke 15:10 God upon one sinner doing penance,** what do we think their joy must be when they see thousands of holy souls joining their company?

And this is also a great celebration for the patriarchs, the prophets, and the other holy souls who today enter for the first time into their supernal native land. If we celebrate a feast for just one saint who gains heaven, how much more should we celebrate for so many thousands of them, and indeed for the saint of saints himself? This is also a great feast for our Lady, for she saw with her own eyes her only-begotten son, in the body that he had received from her, ascend gloriously as true God far beyond the most exalted creatures, exercising by right dominion over all the heavens, and finally reaching the throne next to God the Father. And it is our great feast, too: today our human nature is exalted above the heavens, and through the Lord Jesus ruined humankind is restored to companionship with the angels and enters the heavenly Kingdom. Great indeed is this solemn day, and any soul who loves the Lord Jesus well should rightly rejoice on this day.

Pope Leo writes,

> The Lord Jesus told his disciples: *"If you loved me you would indeed be glad, because I go to the Father."** This ascension is advantageous to you: your lowliness is raised in me above all the heavens and placed at the right hand of the Father. I have united you to myself and have become the Son of Man so that you might become sons and daughters of God.* Because Christ's ascension is our promotion, and because where the glory of the Head has preceded us there we hope that the Body will also be called, let us exult, dearly beloved, with fitting joy and be glad with holy thanksgiving.
>
> Today we are not only established as the possessors of Paradise, but we have even penetrated the heights of the heavens in Christ, prepared more fully for it through the ineffable grace of Christ that we had lost through the devil's hatred. Those whom the violent enemy cast down from the happiness of the first dwelling, the Son of God has incorporated into himself and placed at the Father's right hand.*

*John 14:28

*Sermo 77.5;
PL 54:414AB

*Sermo 73.4;
PL 54:396C

Augustine says,

Today, brethren, as you have heard, the Lord Jesus
Christ ascended to heaven; let our hearts ascend
with him. Just as he did not leave us when he
ascended, let us also be with him, even though
what he has promised has not yet been fulfilled
in our bodies. When he ascended to heaven, we
were not separated from him. He does not be-
grudge us heaven, but in a manner of speaking
he cries out, "If you want to ascend to heaven, be
my members!" Let us all draw strength from this,
let this enkindle our prayerful desires, let this be
our meditation on earth, so that in time we may
be counted among those in heaven. Let us put off
now an aged soul, and later we will put off mortal
flesh. The body will rise easily to the heights of
heaven if the spirit is not weighed down by the
baggage of sin.*

*Sermo
263.2; PL
38:1210–11

And again, "Since we are bereaved of Christ's
presence in time, let us hasten wholeheartedly to the
eternal vision of him and say to him, *'My heart has said
to you: My face has sought you: your face, O Lord, will I
still seek.'** All the labors of Christ's humanity had but
one goal, to direct our attention to heavenly things
and so to lead us at the hour of our death to a clear
vision of him and, having brought us there, to satisfy
us with the eternal glory of his face."* And elsewhere,
"The reason for this solemnity is that we believe that
Christ already reigns at the Father's right hand, and
that during this interval we follow after him on the
wings of hope and charity, as it were. Then, when he
hands over the kingdom to God the Father, we will
reign with him forever.* Let us during this time ascend
with Christ in our hearts, so that when the promised
day arrives we may follow him also in our bodies."*

And, last, Gregory tells us, "Dearly beloved, it is
fitting that we should follow in our hearts to where

*Ps 26:8

*Sermo 47,
author
unknown;
PL 57:628D–
629A

*Sermo 11.3,
author un-
known; PL
54:500
*Ps-Augus-
tine, Sermo
177.1; PL
39:2082

we profess he has ascended in his body. Let us flee
earthly desires, let nothing here below delight us who
have a Father in heaven. If the weakness of our body
still holds us here, let us nevertheless follow him by
the footsteps of our love. He who gave us our desire
will not desert us, Jesus Christ our Lord."*

*40 hom
29.11; PL
76:1219B–D

Christ ascended so that by departing bodily he
might draw our attention from this world and we
would desire him with undivided heart. Therefore,
let us strive for what is on high in our minds and
savor what is on high in our affections.

Types of the Lord's Ascension

Christ's ascension was prefigured by Jacob's
ladder: one end touched the ground and the other
reached heaven, and the angels ascended and descended on it.* Thus did Christ come down from
heaven and ascend back there when he wanted to
reunite earthly and heavenly things. The mediator
between God and humanity had to be himself both
God and Man; otherwise he would not be able to
restore peace between us and God. God is the Most
High, and we are the lowest, so Christ became a
ladder between heaven and earth. The angels come
down this ladder carrying God's grace to us, and they
ascend to heaven carrying our souls there.

*Gen 28:12

Christ also foretold the ascension in his parable
of the one sheep out of a hundred that was lost and
found.* The one sheep was lost when our first parents
transgressed God's command, but God left the other
ninety-nine—that is, the nine choirs of angels—and
came into this world to search for the one lost sheep.
This he did for thirty-three years, laboring so much
that his whole body was covered with bloody sweat.
He put the lost sheep on his shoulders and carried
it when he bore the cross on his back because of our

*Luke 15:3-7

sins. He invited his friends to share in his joy when he ascended together with redeemed humanity, and the whole heavenly court rejoiced.

2 Kgs 2:11 The Lord's ascension was also prefigured by Elijah's departure. Elijah proclaimed the law of God in Judea and boldly admonished transgressors. For this, he was mercilessly persecuted by his enemies but was judged worthy by God to be carried off to Paradise. Likewise, Christ taught the way of truth in Judea and had to endure much persecution from the people there. However, *God also has exalted him and*

Phil 2:9 has given him a name which is above all names. In truth, *Christ had to have suffered these things and so to enter*

Luke 24:26 into his glory. And should we not all the more put up with suffering and distress for the sake of life eternal?

O Jesus, you received a more eminent crown when, after your resurrection, you ascended to the right hand of the Father. Draw my soul to you so that I may desire and seek you alone. Grant, I beseech you, that all my longing and effort may be directed to where I profess you have ascended; may my body alone be detained in this vale of tears, while my thoughts and deepest desires are with you; then my heart will be where you are, O treasure worthy of all my love. Draw me after you, so that through your grace I may ascend from strength to strength and so be found worthy to see you, the God of gods, in Sion. Amen.

15

Pentecost: A Novena

Acts 2:1-13

Ludolph's meditation on Pentecost presents a concise spiritual treatise on the Holy Spirit. This chapter can be read as a whole, but the translator has divided it into sections to serve as a Novena between the Ascension and Pentecost.

First Day: Waiting for the Holy Spirit

And they adoring went back into Jerusalem with great joy,* because all the mysteries had been fulfilled in Christ. They rejoiced at the glorification of their Lord and God, who they knew had entered the heavens after his resurrection, and at the redemption of the whole human race; they rejoiced at the expulsion of the demons and the restoration of the places left vacant by the fallen angels, they rejoiced at the shame brought on Jesus' enemies and the promise of the Holy Spirit, and they rejoiced at the exaltation of human nature and the certain hope of a general resurrection and ascension in the future. Because the Head of the Body had risen and ascended, they treasured a sure hope that the members of his Body would do the same.

    *Luke 24:52

Then the apostles came down with the mother of the Lord and the other women and disciples, and they retired to the Upper Room on Mount Sion to await the promise of the Father, as the Lord had commanded them. During the days between the ascension and Pentecost, blessed Matthias was elected to take the place of Judas among the apostles. *All these*

166   *"Your Hearts Will Rejoice"*

were persevering with one mind in constant and insistent
*Acts 1:14   *prayer* at fitting times. They prepared themselves
daily through prayer so that they would be worthy
to receive the promised Holy Spirit.

And they were always in the temple, praising and
Luke 24:53   blessing God. They were* there *always in the temple,*
which is the place of prayer, *praising and blessing God*
for his benefits, glorifying him for his divine promises, and praying earnestly to receive the gift of the
Holy Spirit. Or, they were *praising* God for his in-
herent goodness and the glorification and ascension
of the Lord, *and blessing God* with thanksgiving for
the bestowal of his benefits, the promise of the Holy
Spirit, and the consolation they had received from the
angels. Nothing distracted them; ignoring everything
else, they persevered in praising God, to await in
that place of prayer the promised coming of the Holy
Spirit, their hearts eager and ready. They alternated
periods of prayer in the temple with times of rest in
the Upper Room.

Let us imitate them, passing this holy life constantly *praising and blessing God.* We, too, will be
found worthy to be raised up by a daily blessing,
if by the daily recollection of Christ's triumphant
ascent into heaven we are *praising and blessing God* in
Jerusalem, that is, if we find rest in the desired and
hoped-for vision of supernal peace. Praying ardently
that we may be able to receive God's gifts, we shall be
like to men who wait for their lord, when he shall return
Luke 12:36   from the wedding.
Bede says,

> So that they might be worthy of the heavenly
> promises, *they were always in the temple, praising*
> *and blessing God.* They were surely aware that the
> Holy Spirit deigns to visit and inhabit only those
> hearts that he sees are devoted to frequenting the
> place of prayer and dedicated to divine praise

and blessing. Hence we read of them in the Acts, *All these were persevering with one mind in prayer.* We must meticulously imitate this description of the apostolic work: we who have the heavenly promises and are commanded to offer insistent supplication to receive them should all come together to adore, and persist in prayer, and as one devoutly entreat the Lord. Nor should we doubt that our loving Creator will deign to hear us if we pray in this way. He will pour forth the grace of his Spirit into our hearts, too, and cause our eyes to be blessed, although not in the same way as those of the apostles, who were found worthy to see the Lord when he was sojourning in the world, teaching, and performing miracles, and when, after his triumph over death, he rose and returned to heaven.

But they will certainly be blessed like the eyes of those about whom he spoke to Thomas the apostle: *"Because you have seen me, Thomas, you have believed; blessed are they that have not seen and have believed."** All believers, whether they were born in the time before his incarnation or they saw him in the flesh, or those like us who live after his ascension, all believers share in that most cheerful promise he made: *"Blessed are the clean of heart: they shall see God."**

*John 20:29

*Matt 5:8;
Hom ev 9
[2.15]; PL
94:177C–178B

Second Day: The Descent of the Holy Spirit

And when the days of the Pentecost were accomplished, that is, fifty days after the resurrection and at the outset of the seven days of Pentecost, *they were all together in one place,** in the Upper Room on Mount Sion where the Last Supper had been held. There were about one hundred and twenty disciples of both sexes gathered, persevering in prayer and awaiting the promise of the Holy Spirit. The number of the apostles had increased tenfold.

*Acts 2:1

˙Acts 2:2

And suddenly, at the third hour, *there came a* crashing *sound* like thunder *from heaven*, that is, from the air, *as of a mighty wind coming*˙ like a powerful breath. The words *as of a mighty wind from heaven* can refer both to the sound from heaven and to the Holy Spirit: he comes with a powerful noise to terrify the rebellious, and as a breath proceeding from deep within to give life to the affections of the devout.

˙Acts 2:4
˙John 3:8

And they were all filled with the Holy Spirit; and they began to speak in various tongues by the impetus of the same Holy Spirit, *according as the Holy Spirit gave them to speak.*˙ *The Spirit breathes where he wills,*˙ and when he wills, and as much as he wills, and how he wills, and on whom he wills. He instructed them all with the truth of luminous understanding, enkindled in them all an unquenchable fire of charity, and strengthened them all with invincible fortitude. He inspired them with the knowledge of all languages. At that time, the church consisted of only one race; that they could speak in the tongues of all people signified that as the church spread to all the nations, she would speak every language, because the church already has all languages. The fact that they could speak all languages shows that all languages would come to believe.

The appearance of the creature by which the Holy Spirit visibly descended expressed the purpose for which he then came upon the apostles: to supply a word to the mouth, a light to the mind, a fire to the affections, and a strength to the heart. The tongue produces words, while fire illuminates, warms, and hardens clay. The Spirit's other purpose, the remission of sins, was given after the resurrection, when Christ breathed on his apostles and said, *"Receive the Holy Spirit. Whose sins you shall forgive, they are forgiven them, and whose sins you shall retain, they are retained."*˙

˙John
20:22-23

Here we should note that the Holy Spirit was sent twice upon Christ and twice upon the apostles. He

came upon Christ in the form of a dove at his baptism and in the form of a cloud at his transfiguration.
The grace of Christ, which is given through the Holy
Spirit, must be obtained by us in two ways: through
the propagation of grace in the sacraments, so the
Spirit descended in the form of a dove, which is a
prolific animal, and through teaching, so the Spirit
descended in the form of a luminous cloud, revealing
Christ as teacher: *Hear him.*˙ He descended upon the
apostles first in a breath to signify the propagation
of grace in the sacraments, of which they were to
be the ministers, when it was said, *"Whose sins you
shall forgive, they are forgiven them,"* and in the form
of tongues of fire to signify the propagation of grace
through teaching, so that after *they were all filled with
the Holy Spirit, they began to speak in various tongues.*
Gregory says,

˙Luke 9:35

> We read that the apostles clearly received the
> Holy Spirit twice: the first time when the Lord
> was still abiding on earth, through his breathing
> on them; the second time after the Lord took his
> place in heaven, in various tongues through fire.
> Charity, which is diffused into hearts by the Holy
> Spirit, contains two precepts: love of God and love
> of neighbor. The Spirit is given on earth so that
> the neighbor will be loved, and the Spirit is given
> from heaven so that God will be loved. Just as
> there is one charity and two commandments, so
> there is one Spirit and two gifts. Love of neighbor
> leads to love of God, so it was proper that the
> Holy Spirit should be given first on earth and later
> from heaven. Hence John asks, *"For he that loves
> not his brother whom he sees, how can he love God
> whom he does not see?"*˙

˙1 John 4:20;
40 hom 26.3;
PL 76:1198D–
1198A

In addition, the Holy Spirit was also given to the
apostles before the passion to cleanse them when
they were baptized and to empower them to perform

miracles when they were sent out to preach and were told, *"Heal the sick, raise the dead, cleanse the lepers, cast out devils."** Jerome says,

*Matt 10:8

> I forthrightly declare that the apostles always had the Holy Spirit from the time they came to believe in Christ. They would not have been able to perform signs without his grace. However, they received him in degrees according to their capacity. On the first day of the resurrection they received that grace of the Holy Spirit by which they could forgive sins, baptize, and give the Spirit of adoption to believers. Then on the day of Pentecost there was the fulfillment of a greater promise: they received power from on high to preach Christ's Gospel to all the nations.*

*Ep 120.9; PL 22:994

And Leo writes, "Let us not call into question that when the Holy Spirit filled the Lord's disciples at Pentecost, this was not the beginning of a gift but an addition to his generosity. The patriarchs, prophets, priests, and all the holy ones who lived in former times were invigorated by the sanctification of the same Holy Spirit. Without this grace, no sacraments would ever have been established, no mysteries celebrated—the same power of charisms was always at work, although there was not the same measure of gifts."*

*Sermo 76.3; PL 54:405C– 406A

Third Day: The Visible and Invisible Missions of the Holy Spirit

When the Holy Spirit is given, he can be sent either visibly or invisibly. He comes visibly when there is some sign of his presence. He revealed his presence tangibly in five ways: first, in the form of dove hovering over Christ at his baptism; second, as a luminous cloud overshadowing Christ at his transfiguration; third, as a breath, when Jesus breathed

on his disciples and gave them the Holy Spirit on
Easter; fourth and fifth, in the appearance of fire and
tongues, the two forms in which he appeared on this
day. He is sent invisibly when he flows into chaste
souls to sanctify his creatures, as it says: *The Spirit
breathes where he will and you hear his voice; but you do
not know where he comes from or where he goes.*   *John 3:8
   Bernard teaches,

> The invisible Word does not come in through the
> eyes, for he has no color; nor through the ears, for
> he makes no sound; nor through the nostrils, for
> he does not mingle with the air but with the mind;
> nor through the jaws, for he cannot be chewed
> or swallowed; nor through the touch, for he is
> not palpable.* So you ask, "If his ways are not   *SC 74.5; PL
> discernible, how will I know he is present?" To be   183:1141B
> sure, I have known his presence from the move-
> ment of my heart; I have known his strength when
> I have fled from carnal attachments and vices;
> I have been filled with wonder at the depth of
> wisdom from the revelation of my secrets; I have
> experienced his gentle kindness in the slightest
> improvement in my behavior; I have perceived
> something of his beauty in the spiritual renewal
> of my mind; and, contemplating all of this at once,
> I have stood in awe at his manifold greatness.*   *SC 74.6; PL
183:1141D–
1142A

And Chrysostom says, "We can know that the
Holy Spirit dwells in us if we are thinking about
something good; if we think about something evil,
it is a sign that the Holy Spirit has withdrawn from
us."* Augustine writes,   *Jerome,
Com Mark
1:11; CCL
78:459, lines
265–66

> In early times the Holy Spirit descended on be-
> lievers and they spoke languages they had not
> learned, as the Holy Spirit gave them to pro-
> nounce. The signs were suited to the time, for it
> was necessary to signify the Holy Spirit with all
> tongues because the Gospel of God was about to

travel by all languages to every part of the world. That sign was made, and it passed away. If the presence of the Holy Spirit is no longer manifested by such miracles, how does it occur? How do you know whether you have received the Holy Spirit? Question your heart. If you love your brother and sister, the Spirit of God abides in you. Examine yourself before the eyes of God; see if there is in you a love of unity of peace, and a love for the church spread throughout the whole world. Take care not to love only the person in front of you: we do not see many sisters and brothers, but we are united to them in the unity of the Spirit. What cause is there to marvel that they are not with us? We are in one body; we have one head in heaven.*

*Tr John ep 6.10; PL 35:2025

So, if you want to know if you have received the Holy Spirit, ask your heart: if fraternal charity is there, you can rest easy, for there can be no love without the Holy Spirit. As Paul says, *"the charity of God is poured forth in our hearts, by the Holy Spirit who is given to us."**

*Rom 5:5; Tr John ep 6.10; PL 35:2025

The invisible mission of the Holy Spirit occurs by his dwelling in a rational creature; the visible mission occurs to make that indwelling known to others.

Fourth Day: Signs of the Spirit's Presence

We cannot be absolutely certain that the Holy Spirit is present in someone, because *the Spirit breathes where he will, but you do not know where he comes from and where he goes.** There are signs, however, that allow us to conjecture that the Holy Spirit is present or absent, and these differ according to three states: beginners, the proficient, and the perfect. The Holy Spirit acts differently in people according to the needs of each state, and for this reason the signs of his presence differ. The Holy Spirit breathes, inhabits, and fills: he breathes in beginners, dwells in the proficient, and fills the perfect.

*John 3:8

There are three signs that the Holy Spirit breathes in a beginner. The first, according to Bernard, is sorrow for past sins, because the Holy Spirit hates impurities and cannot dwell in a body subject to sin.* The second is a firm and efficacious intention to avoid future sins, which none of us can have of our own unaided power without the Holy Spirit's assisting us with grace and helping us in our weakness. The third is promptness in doing good; according to Gregory, the love of God (which is the Holy Spirit) is never idle; if it is present, it does great things.*

*In festo Pent 3.5; PL 183:332B

*40 hom 30.2; PL 76:1221B

There are three signs that suggest the Holy Spirit is dwelling in the proficient. The first is a frequent, careful examination of conscience—and not just of mortal sins, but of venial as well. Just as the Holy Spirit opposes mortal sins, so the fervor of charity, which comes from the Holy Spirit, opposes venial sins and drives them from the soul, lest the Holy Spirit be displeased. The second is a weakening of concupiscence: to the extent that charity continues to grow in the proficient, to that extent their hearts are withdrawn from temporal concerns. The third is a zealous observance of the commandments, because it is not possible to keep the commandments without true love. Augustine gives this example: "Who could say, 'I love the emperor but I hate his laws'? If you say that you love God, keep his commandments."*

*Tr John ep 9.11; PL 35:2053

Then there are the three signs that suggest that the Holy Spirit fills the perfect. The first is the manifestation of divine truth. Because the Holy Spirit is the Spirit of truth, it pertains to him to teach all truth: thus, if he is in a person, he will make known some divine mysteries, sharing them as with an intimate friend. The second sign is to fear nothing but God alone. *Perfect charity casts out fear,* for it has no punishment, but fear has punishment. Hence the apostle says, *"Where the Spirit of the Lord is, there is liberty,"**

*1 John 4:18

*2 Cor 3:17

and liberty does not remain with servile fear. The third sign is a desire to depart from here: someone has such an intense love for God that he wants to die and be with Christ because the Holy Spirit lifts his mind to supernal desires. Happy is that soul who desires to die and be with Christ, for this is the most certain sign that the Holy Spirit fills her.

Finally there are three visible signs of Holy Spirit's indwelling. He appeared in the form of a cloud over Christ at his transfiguration, he appeared in the form of a dove over Christ at his baptism, and he appeared in the form of fire over the apostles when they were gathered together as a group. The first sign is an abundance of tears: he appeared in the form of a cloud, which, when it comes from the south, produces rain; so, when the Spirit comes, the soul pours out tears. The second sign is the forgetting of injuries: he appeared as a dove, which is without gall. The third sign is a longing for higher things: he appeared as flame, which tends to rise up, and so the Holy Spirit raises our hearts on high.

Fifth Day: The Worldly Cannot Receive the Holy Spirit

Now there were dwelling at Jerusalem Jews, devout men, many of whom came *out of every nation under heaven.** Many Jews had been dispersed in various captivities, but they now came together by God's command for the feast. When they heard the peal of thunder and the mighty wind that sounded in the air above the Upper Room, they all gathered around the disciples and marveled *that every man heard them speak in his own tongue. But others mocking, said: "These men are full of new wine."** Although they said this in jest, in fact they spoke the truth: the disciples were not full of the old wine that had been served at the

*Acts 2:5

*Acts 2:6, 13

wedding feast, but of the new vintage of spiritual grace, of which it is said elsewhere, *"No man puts new wine into old bottles."**

*Luke 5:37

Then Peter stood up with the eleven, showing that they were not drunk, for it was *but the third hour of the day,** not yet the time to eat. Rather, they were filled with the Holy Spirit, for it had been prophesied by Joel that the Holy Spirit would come upon men. Then Christ, who had ascended, *gave gifts to men,** that is, the Holy Spirit; for all of our goods are from above, where he ascended. What he had promised before his passion was fulfilled: *"If I go not, the Paraclete will not come to you; but if I go, I will send him to you."**

*Acts 2:15

*Eph 4:8

*John 16:7

Bernard says,

> The apostles, still clinging to the Lord's flesh (which was uniquely holy, inasmuch as it belonged to the Holy of holies) were unable to be filled with the Holy Spirit until it was taken away from them. Do you imagine that you, who are bound and inseparably attached to your own flesh, which is sordid and full of filthy images, can receive that most truthful Spirit unless you have tried to renounce those carnal comforts at their root? To be sure, sorrow will fill your heart when you begin; but if you persevere, your sorrow will turn to joy. Then your affections will be purified and your will renewed, or, rather, recreated. Then you will hasten with pleasure and eagerness through everything that seemed extremely difficult or even impossible before.*

*Sermo in Asc 3.8; PL 183:308AB

Therefore, if you long for spiritual delights you must spurn those of the flesh, for, as Gregory says, "As soon as we tear away something of the flesh, we find something in the spirit that gives delight."*

*Mor 30.10.39; PL 76:546C

We can distinguish between spiritual and carnal people from the words of the apostle: *"They that are according to the flesh mind the things that are of the flesh,*

*Rom 8:5

but they that are according to the spirit mind the things that are of the spirit." More specifically, spiritual people exhibit the following traits: they are as prompt at fleeing from situations where they can be injured spiritually as they are from places where they can be harmed physically; they strive as willingly to heal the soul as the body—for, as the soul is more worthy than the body, so it is more important to avoid injuring the soul than the body.

Again, they find that spiritual food, be it prayer, preaching, Scripture, spiritual reading, the Body of Christ, or the Divine Office, delights and comforts their soul as much as material food does their body, and they are as unwilling to disregard the time for taking spiritual nourishment as they are to neglect meal time. Again, they will be as diligent about the spirit as carnal persons are about the body. Worldly people are very solicitous to have what they need at any given time, summer and winter, in the way of clothing and food. Spiritual persons should be concerned about the grace they need in times of prosperity and adversity, what they require in regard to friends and enemies, how they should comport themselves when they are alone with God and when they are in the company of others, and so on.

*Sir 31:9

But *who is he, and we will praise him?* Although people in our day do good, they do it in half measures. Some have secured the grace to be generous with alms, but they fall into sins of the flesh; others are chaste in body but burn with the passion of greed; others have the grace of gentleness, but their rancor of soul makes them mean-spirited; others are quick to forgive injuries done to them and forget them, but they are less cautious about their own heart and quickly provoke violent quarrels with their anger; God has been generous with others, but then they boast as if it were all their own doing; others weaken their bodies by abstaining from food, but they consume pride, avarice, envy, and other wicked things, or they disparage their brother as if they were devouring his flesh and blood. It can truly be said of many today, *"He that is best among them is as a brier; and he that is righteous, as the thorn of the hedge."**   *Mic 7:4

There are many things required if we want to make progress and serve God in the spiritual life: first, a clear, perfect awareness of our own weaknesses and defects; second, a powerful, fervent anger directed against our wicked natural desires and inclinations; third, a great fear because of the offenses we have committed against God to date, for we cannot be certain that we have made complete satisfaction for them and so are at peace with God; fourth, a similar fear in regard to ourselves, lest in our weakness we return to the same sins or even worse ones; fifth, drastic amendment and firm control over our five senses and our entire body, submitting it entirely to the service of Jesus Christ; sixth, shunning completely like an infernal demon any person or other creature that persuades us not only to commit sin but to allow any imperfection in the spiritual life; seventh, a continuous, sweet recollection in a spirit of thanksgiving of God's blessings received until now, and those that come to us every day from the Lord Jesus Christ; eighth, to remain at prayer night and day; ninth, to carry Christ's cross ourselves, which has four arms: mortification for mortal sins, abandonment of all temporal goods, cutting off carnal attachments to friends, and self-contempt and abasement.

Sixth Day: The Effects of the Holy Spirit

The disciples were few in number and very ordinary, but once they had been illuminated and instructed, inflamed and assisted, comforted and strengthened, consoled and filled with every joy by the power of the Holy Spirit, they shook up the whole world and in great part conquered it. Partly by words of fire, partly by perfect examples, and partly by wondrous prodigies, they planted the church everywhere in the world. The church, purified, illuminated, and perfected by the power of the Holy Spirit, became lovable and splendidly arrayed to her bridegroom, but to Satan and his angels, she is *terrible as an army set in array.*˙

˙Song 6:3

But they going forth preached everywhere, with the Lord working and confirming the word with signs that followed.˙ In accordance with Christ's mandate, however, they did not set out immediately after his ascension, but waited until they received the Holy Spirit. Indeed, they remained in Judea for about twelve years; then, after preaching there, they made a solemn division of the world and went forth. They separated and, *going forth, preached everywhere* in the world what must be understood, believed, done, and desired; *with the Lord working,* without whom they could do nothing, supplying the strength for their work, *and confirming the word with signs that followed,* so that by the power of the name of Jesus they could command every creature and sickness.

˙Mark 16:20

They performed miraculous signs to give firm credence to their teaching; a message that is beyond nature and reason must be confirmed by signs. Gregory comments, "Obedience followed the command, and signs followed their obedience."˙˙ Back then, preaching was confirmed by miraculous signs; today, preachers should confirm their preaching with good works. Theophylact writes, "We must also know from this that now words are confirmed by deeds, just as in those days the apostles confirmed their words *with signs that followed.* Grant then, O Christ, that the words we speak about virtue may be confirmed by

˙40 hom 29.8;
PL 76:1217D

works and deeds, so that at the last, with your assistance, we may be perfect in word and deed: for
renown is due to you for words and deeds, because
you are the power and wisdom of God forever and
ever." *

Then the prophecy was fulfilled: *"Their sound has
gone forth into all the earth, and their words unto the
ends of the world."* * The fiery, sanctifying Spirit sowed
words in the hearts of the apostles: like a virtuoso,
he filled the twelve pipes of faith's organ with new
wind so that as he played various spiritual modula-
tions through the apostles he could scatter abroad
the words of divine virtue, attracting all nations by
the delightful sound and proclaiming the mystery
of the Trinity.

The impact and significant fruit produced by
the Holy Spirit indicates with what great veneration
this solemnity should be celebrated today. Gregory
exhorts us, "Consider, dearly beloved, after the incarnation of the Only Begotten Son of God, today's
solemn observance of the coming of the Holy Spirit.
Like that event, this one too is worthy of honor. In
the former, God, while remaining in himself, received
a man; in this, men and women receive God, who
comes from above. In the former, God became man
by nature; in this, men and women become gods by
adoption.* Ponder how great is this solemnity, to have
God come as a guest into our heart. Let those who
are preparing a home in their souls for God sweep
out the dirt of evil deeds." *

Here we should note that the Lord Jesus did not
send the Holy Spirit immediately after his ascension,
but ten days later: first, so that the apostles could prepare themselves for his coming by prayer and fasting;
second, because only those who had fulfilled the Ten
Commandments could receive the Holy Spirit. He
sent the Spirit fifty days after the resurrection: just

*En ev Mark
16:14-20; PG
123:682

*Ps 18:5

*40 hom 30.9;
PL 76:1226B

*40 hom 30.2;
PL 76:1220D–
1221A

as the Jewish people had received the law of fear
fifty days after their liberation from Egypt, so the
faithful received the law of love fifty days after their
liberation from the earth. Also, in the jubilee, that
is, every fiftieth year, the Jews recovered their lost
liberty and inheritance, and on this day the Christian
people received their lost liberty and their inheritance
of Paradise. At Pentecost, the Jews celebrate the Lord
descending in flames on Mount Sinai to give the law
to all who heard it. Therefore, on the fiftieth day after
Passover, the Holy Spirit descended in tongues of
flame upon the disciples on Mount Sion.

Bede writes,

> Obviously this solemnity is not consecrated only
> to the Gospel charisms but also to the myster-
> ies of the law that once foreshadowed them and
> were observed by annual ceremonies at the Lord's
> command.˙ When the children of Israel had been
> freed from slavery in Egypt by the sacrifice of the
> paschal lamb, they went into the desert to reach
> the Promised Land, and they made their way to
> Mount Sinai. On the fiftieth day after Passover the
> Lord came down in fire on the mountain to give
> them the law, and, to commemorate the giving of
> the law, he decreed that on that day every year
> they should bring to the altar a sacrifice of first
> fruits for him.
>
> The meaning of the immolation of the paschal
> lamb and the deliverance from slavery in Egypt
> are evident to all who read about them: *Christ
> our pasch is sacrificed.*˙ He himself is the true Lamb
> who took away the sins of the world, who has
> redeemed us from slavery at the price of his own
> blood, and by the precedent of his resurrection
> he has shown us the hope of life and perpetual
> freedom. The law was given when the Lord came
> down onto the mountain in fire on the fiftieth day
> after the slaying of the lamb; in the same way,
> fifty days after our Redeemer's resurrection the

˙Hom ev
2.11; PL
94:193C

˙1 Cor 5:7

grace of the Holy Spirit was given to the disciples
while they were gathered together in the Upper
Room. The elevation of the Cenacle and the summit of the mountain indicate the sublimity of the
heavenly precepts and gifts. No one who clings
to base desires can comply with the divine commandments or be worthy of gifts from on high.*

*Hom ev
2.11; PL
94:194A–C

Seventh Day: The Holy Spirit Inspires Us to Love Heavenly Things

Let us hasten to enter into that eternal repose
where endless joys abound; let us sigh from our ef-
forts to attain our heavenly homeland. We are sad
while we are in the world because *we are absent from
the Lord*: whoever is not absent from the body is absent from the Lord. It would be much better to be
away from the body and cling to the Lord. As the
apostle says, *"While we are in the body we are absent
from the Lord."** Let us say with this same apostle, *"I
have a desire to be dissolved and to be with Christ."** And,
*"Unhappy man that I am, who shall deliver me from the
body of this death?"**

*2 Cor 5:6
*Phil 1:23

*Rom 7:24

Let us long for this dissolution and beg the Lord
for it continually, for we cannot attain it ourselves.
And in the meantime, let us die to the displays of the
world and with a resolute heart distance ourselves
from these perishable things, these momentary miser-
ies and the paltry consolations. According to Gregory,
those who love visible things forfeit invisible ones.*
Leo teaches, "What the outer person enjoys is what
most corrupts the inner person; the rational soul is
purified to the degree that the bodily flesh is chastised."* Or briefly, in the words of Augustine, "Let
other creatures become worthless so that the Creator
alone becomes sweet in the heart."*

*Mor 21.2.4;
PL 76:190C

*Sermo 78.1;
PL 54:416B

*Sermo 279.1;
PL 38:1276

The apostle writes, *"The creature was made subject to vanity."** This being so, it plays its lovers false

*Rom 8:20

and deceives many who are not on guard. O, how happy is the person whom the miserable vanities of the world do not seduce, which especially in these days delude so many! Chrysostom exhorts us,

*Eccl 1:2

> It can always be said, but now more than ever: *"Vanity of vanities, and all is vanity."** Would that those who dwell in powerful positions understood this little phrase and inscribed it on all the walls and doors of their houses, on their clothing, and above all in their consciences, so that they would have it continually before their eyes and feel it in their hearts! There are so many appearances and false images that deceive the unwary that we need to sing this same melody daily, at every lunch and dinner. In every gathering whatsoever, we should sing to our neighbors and gladly hear from them in turn, *"Vanity of vanities, and all is vanity."**

*Eutropium
1; PG 52:391

Therefore, let us transfer our love from passing things to those that are incorruptible; called to what is heavenly, let us find our delight in what is higher. Let us rejoice in what brings joy to the saints, desiring their riches and aspiring to attain them by imitating their example; if we are sharers in their devotion, we will have fellowship in their dignity. As Augustine observes about Christ, *"he has rejoiced as a giant to run*

*Ps 18:6

*the way,** for he did not tarry but ran, crying out by words, deeds, death, life, descending, ascending, so that we would return to him, and he departed from our sight so that we would return to our heart, and

*Conf 4.12.19;
PL 32:701

there find him."*

Keeping our eyes fixed on the Lord and treasuring him continually in our heart, let us fight valiantly, for this present life is a campaign, a conflict, and a battle: prosperity and adversity, fervor and tepidity, eating and fasting, sleep and vigil, anxiety and laziness, weeping and joy, rest and labor, health and sickness, pain and pleasure, and whatever else there may be in this world lay traps for us and do battle with us. Our soul must always be on guard, because it never lacks a scheming adversary; our struggle is brief, but the reward is eternal. And we cannot stop fighting: no matter how victorious we have been, there will always be another foe to vanquish. Leo warns, "Although divine grace gives daily victories to his saints, he does not take away the substance of the struggle. This is in fact another mercy from our protector: he wanted to leave something for our changeable nature to overcome, lest battle concluded be an occasion for pride."* And Chrysostom says, "Even though the saints cannot be overcome by the flesh because they are already spiritual, they can still be assaulted because they are still carnal."*

*Sermo 78.2; PL 54:417A

*Opus imperf, hom 35; PG 56:825

Eighth Day: The Holy Spirit Strengthens Us in Adversity

Therefore, whatever momentary delight or anguish should occur, let us think of it as already passed and direct our gaze to what abides forever. All things in this world pass as quickly as a shadow, so they should be considered to be in the past or not to have happened at all. What pleases or causes anguish here is gone in no time, but what pleases or causes anguish later lasts. We cannot enjoy or endure here anything comparable to what we will enjoy or endure in the life to come. Bernard says, *"The sufferings of this time are not worthy to be compared with*"* the sins we committed, the benefits we receive, the pains of hell we avoid, and the eternal reward we anticipate."*

*Rom 8:18

*De conv 37, approx; PL 182:855B

Chrysostom exhorts us,

Let us do all things so as not to be deprived of glory. This is not difficult to accomplish if we desire it, nor is it arduous if we apply ourselves. *If*

*2 Tim 2:12

we suffer, we shall also reign with him. If we suffer
what? If we bear with tribulation and persecution,
if we walk in the narrow way. The narrow way is
difficult, but the hope of future things makes our
choice easier. Let us turn our gaze toward heaven,
picturing and seeing what is there. If we always
dwell on those things, we will not suffer from
earthly delights here, nor will the world's sorrows
be too heavy to bear. We will laugh at such things,
and nothing will have the power either to depress
or exalt us, provided that our sole desire leads
there and contemplates that love.

What am I saying? Spiritual love is such that
we will not feel pain in present difficulties nor
be able to see future ones. When loved ones are
absent, we picture them every day; so great is
love's tyranny that it gives up everything else and
binds the soul fast to the object of our affection. If
we loved Christ like that, everything here would
be but shadows, illusions, and dreams. And we
would ask ourselves, *"Who then shall separate us
from the love of Christ? Shall tribulation? Or distress?
Or famine? Or nakedness? Or danger? Or persecution? Or the sword?"* The apostle did not say,
"Shall money? Or riches? Or beauty?" for these
are so worthless as to be laughable. Rather, he
mentioned things that are truly painful: famine,
persecution, death; and even these he spits out as
meaningless. Reflecting on all this, and comparing
delights with delights, let us choose those that are
better so that we can enjoy future goods.

*Rom 8:35

*Hom John
87.3; PG
59:476

Ninth Day: The Holy Spirit Enables Us
to Praise God

*Ps 117:24

Therefore, we should praise the Lord with all our
might on this feast. *Let us be glad and rejoice therein,*
for, having come to the faith, we have gained no in-
significant fruit. And not only has the whole human

race found reason for joy in this solemnity, but the Blessed Virgin also received more joy from it. Anselm writes,

> The magnitude of her joys increased greatly when the Holy Spirit came upon the disciples: as soon as they began to preach, a large number of people came to believe in her son. In addition to the joy she felt in them for having conceived the salvation of the human race, she understood that her son had not given his life in vain: she saw how efficacious faith in his death was, even among those who had brought it about.* She saw humanity being called to salvation, which she had previously understood to be the reason that the Son took flesh from her and suffered on the cross. She rejoiced that the hope with which she had earlier conceived had now become a reality. People rejoiced, and rejoice still, because they have regained with a hundredfold interest what they had lost: they fell as slaves, they arise as brothers and sisters, sons and daughters.*

*Eadmer, De exc 6; PL 159:569AB

*Eadmer, Quatuor 8; PL 159:585D–586A

While we should make a special effort to praise God especially on such feasts, in fact we should always and everywhere praise him. As Gregory observes, it is a cause for wonder if we do not continuously praise God, because every creature invites us to praise him.* But the grace of the Holy Spirit is much needed for us to do this. Bernard says, "If people give but little energy to praising God, it is a most certain proof by experience that they do not have the Holy Spirit in them: where the Holy Spirit abides, he stirs up praise for God."* Invoking the Holy Spirit, let us always praise God. This is why we were created: to praise God ceaselessly.

*quoted in Auvergne, 2:190

*Source unknown

The citizens of the heavenly city praise God continually. In that place there are always joyful days and the solemnities never end; thanksgiving and praise are endless, as it is written, *Blessed are they that dwell in your house, O Lord; they shall praise you forever and ever.* It is this that most associates us with heavenly things while we are still pilgrims on earth. Bernard teaches, "Nothing so closely approximates on earth the condition of life in the heavenly dwelling as eagerness to praise God. As it says in the Scriptures, *'Blessed are they that dwell in your house, O Lord; they shall praise you forever and ever.'"*

In order to devote energy to the praise of God, I urge you to turn your thoughts as much as you can from mundane concerns and raise them to heavenly ones. Reflect on how those in the heavenly court continually rejoice, exult, and delight in God. Call to mind the joys of each of them and, to the extent you can, mingle with them and join in their joyful praises.

With all your heart, from the depths of your being, cry out with Anselm,

Now, from this moment, I instruct all my desires: grow fervent and flow to the Lord Jesus; run, for you have hesitated long enough; hurry to where you are going, search for the one you seek. *You seek Jesus of Nazareth, who was crucified.* He has ascended to heaven; *he is not here.* The most beloved of the Lord dwells in security, *nor shall the scourge come near his dwelling.* Above the heights of the heavens, above all the excellence of the angels, he ascended by his own power and sits upon a throne of unique splendor at his Father's right hand, coeternal and consubstantial, clothed with divine light and crowned with glory and honor as befits the Only-Begotten of God, serene in joy and almighty in power, Lord in heaven and on earth.

Jesus, generous giver of all gifts, who sent the Holy Spirit upon your disciples in the form of tongues of flame, I humbly beseech you who are so merciful that, unworthy though I am, I too may receive for the sake

*Ps 83:5

*SC 11.1; PL 183:824B

*Mark 16:6

*Ps 90:10

*Eckbert, De Christo [Anselm Med 13]; PL 158:773B

*of my salvation the gifts you lavished on your disci-
ples. Send upon us, your servants, the Spirit of your
charity, goodwill, and peace to visit our hearts: purge
them of wickedness, adorn them with virtues, bind
them with the bond of charity, illuminate them with
the light of your knowledge, and inflame them with the
ardor of your love. Pardon our sins and grant eternal
life. Amen.*

Epilogue

The Romance of the Resurrection

Ludolph has brought us with Christ from the tomb to the glory of heaven. We who live between our Lord's ascension and his glorious return are sustained by two promises: *I am with you always, to the close of the age,** and *I will come again and will take you to myself, that where I am you may be also.** The risen Christ consoles and encourages us on our own roads to Emmaus, but then he disappears again, and we must go in search of him.

*Matt 28:20
*John 14:3

This divine *ludus amoris*, the game of love between God and us, is a mystical theme as ancient as the Song of Songs and as fresh as the seemingly artless yet profound writings of Saint Thérèse. All individuals, whether they know it or not, are involved in this search, for only God can satisfy the deepest longings of the human heart. When the beloved hides himself, this is not to torment us, although it may feel that way at times; rather, he does this to intensify our longing so that we will embrace even more of God's infinite love.

Ludolph concludes his entire *Vita Christi* with a beautiful expression of this romantic quest, the medieval hymn *Iesu dulcis memoria*. Traditionally attributed to Saint Bernard, the hymn was probably written by an English Cistercian in the late twelfth century. It certainly expresses Bernard's fervor as it recounts the lover's relentless pursuit of the beloved, Jesus. The drama of the Song of Songs is transposed into the Easter season, where the appearances and disappearances of the risen Christ fuel the lover's ardor, ending with Christ's ascension to the Father. Like those first disciples, may we catch glimpses of the risen Lord as we walk the road of life, until that day when we behold him forever in glory. There, he promised, *"I will see you again and your hearts will rejoice, and no one will take your joy from you"* *—not even the Lord himself, so tantalizingly elusive now.

*John 16:22

Iesu Dulcis Memoria

JESUS—to think of him brings joy,	*Iesu dulcis memoria,*
True peace of heart without alloy;	*Dans vera cordis gaudia;*
But more than honey and all that's dear?	*Sed super mel et omnia,*
The sweetness of his presence here.	*Eius dulcis praesentia.*
No song can so delight the ear,	*Nihil canitur suavius,*
No voice can bring such welcome cheer,	*Nil auditur iucundius,*
No thought refresh the mind of one	*Nil cogitatur dulcius,*
Like Jesus, God the Father's Son.	*Quam Iesus Dei Filius.*
Jesus, hope of the penitent,	*Iesu, spes poenitentibus,*
Gentle to those who now repent;	*Quam pius es petentibus,*
To those who seek, you are so kind—	*Quam bonus te quaerentibus,*
What must you be to those who find?	*Sed quid invenientibus?*
Jesus, you are the heart's delight,	*Iesu, dulcedo cordium,*
Fountain of life and inward light,	*Fons vivus, lumen mentium,*
Exceeding other joys above,	*Excedis omne gaudium,*
So far surpassing other love.	*Et omne desiderium.*
No human tongue can dare to say,	*Nec lingua valet dicere,*
No feeble pen could e'er portray;	*Nec littera exprimere;*
Experience alone can know	*Expertus potest credere,*
Just what it means to love him so.	*Quid sit Iesum diligere.*

In the bedchamber of my heart
I look for him, the better part—
Within, without, below, above,
In anguish seek the one I love.

With Magdalen on Easter day
I seek the tomb where Jesus lay.
I scrutinize that place apart
Not with my eyes, but with my
  heart.

His absence only feeds my fears,
I bathe his empty tomb with tears.
Then at his sacred feet I fall,
Devoutly hold the Lord of all!

Jesus, most wondrous King of
  kings,
Throughout the world your triumph
  rings!
For you are altogether fair,
Source of all bliss beyond compare.

Remain with us, Redeemer dear,
Upon us shed your brightness here;
Now drive away the dark of night,
And fill the world with joyful light!

For when you dwell within our
  heart
Your light of truth you there impart;
The spell of earthly pride then
  breaks,
And ardent love within awakes.

Jesus' great love for us, so sweet!
Its gentleness, how truly meet!
A thousand times more gracious far
Than e'en our highest praises are.

Iesum quaeram in lectulo,
Clauso cordis cubiculo,
Privatim et in publico;
Quaeram amore sedulo.

Cum Maria, diluculo,
Iesum quaeram in tumulo,
Clamore cordis querulo
Mente quaeram, non oculo.

Tumbam perfundam fletibus,
Locum replens gemitibus;
Iesu provolvar pedibus,
Strictis haerens amplexibus.

Iesu, Rex admirabilis,

Et triumphator nobilis,

Dulcedo ineffabilis,
Totus desiderabilis!

Mane nobiscum, Domine,
Et nos illustra lumine,
Pulsa mentis caligine,
Mundum replens dulcedine.

Quando cor nostrum visitas,

Tunc lucet ei veritas;
Mundi vilescit vanitas;

Et intus fervet caritas.

Amor Iesu dulcissimus,
Et vere suavissimus,
Plus millies gratissimus,
Quam dicere sufficimus.

This his most bitter passion shows,
His precious blood that freely flows;
Through him redemption's truly sealed,
The Father's loving face revealed.

Jesus, then, let all adore,
Let each of us his love implore;
We ardently invoke his name;
Deep longing turns our hearts to flame.

Give him your love, your Lover true,
Return the love he gives to you;
Run close behind his fragrance now,
Vow in your turn what he does vow.

Jesus, the source of tenderness,
Giver of hope and happiness,
Fountain of grace and glory bright,
True source of all my heart's delight!

Good Jesus, let me taste and see
The fullest sweetness that can be;
By your most loving presence here
Let me behold your glory near.

Although my words are far too weak,
Still I find my tongue must speak:
My love conspires to make me bold
Lest my sole joy remain untold.

Jesus, you give with love so kind,
Welcome refreshment to the mind;
You do not loathe to fill entire—
And still we hunger with desire!

Hoc probat eius passio;
Hoc sanguinis effusio,
Per quam nobis redemptio

Datur, et Dei visio.

Iesum omnes agnoscite,
Amorem eius poscite;
Iesum ardenter quaerite,
Quaerendo inardescite.

Sic amantem diligite,

Amoris vicem reddite;
In hunc odorem currite,
Et vota votis reddite.

Iesu, auctor clementiae,
Totius spes laetitiae,
Dulcoris fons et gratiae
Verae cordis deliciae.

Iesu mi bone, sentiam
Tui dulcoris copiam;
Da mihi per praesentiam
Tuam, videre gloriam.

Cum digne loqui nequeam

De te, tamen non sileam;
Amor facit ut audeam,
Cum de te solo gaudeam.

Tua, Iesu, dilectio,
Grata mentis refectio,
Replens sine fastidio,
Dans famem desiderio.

Who taste of you will hunger more,
Who drink be thirsty as before;
They do not know what else to
    seek:
Of Jesus' love alone can speak.

The one your love intoxicates
Knows that Jesus captivates.
How blest the draught that fills his
    store
And makes him want for nothing
    more!

Jesus, angelic joy prolong
In my ear the sweetest song;
On tongue you are the honey best,
Heavenly nectar in the breast!

A thousand hopes that you appear!
When, my Jesus, draw you near?
When will you cause me to rejoice?
When satisfy me with your voice?

Your ardent love, which does not
    cease,
Makes me faint with inner peace;
Sweet fruit that banishes all strife,
Bestower of eternal life.

Jesus, high courtesy untold,
Joy that hearts can always hold,
O sovereign goodness unsurpassed,
May your compassion hold me fast.

(Truly, to love him is most blest,
Jesus himself, my one request;
All else can fade, all else grow
    dim—
I only want to live for him.)

Qui te gustant, esuriunt,
Qui bibunt, adhuc sitiunt;
Desiderare nesciunt,

Nisi Iesum, quem diligunt.

Quem tuus amor ebriat,
Novit quid Iesus sapiat.
Quam felix est quem satiat,

Non est ultra quod cupiat!

Iesu, decus angelicum,
In aure dulce canticum,
In ore mel mirificum,
In corde nectar coelicum!

Desidero te millies,
Iesu mi; quando venies?
Me laetum quando facies?
Me de te quando saties?

Amor tuus continuus,

Mihi languor assiduus,
Mihi fructus mellifluus,
Est et vitae perpetuus.

Iesu, summa benignitas,
Mira cordis jucunditas,
Incomprehensa bonitas,
Tua me stringit caritas.

Bonum mihi diligere
Iesum, nil ultra quaerere;
Mihi prorsus deficere,

Ut illi queam vivere.

You my hope, Jesus most sweet.	*O Iesu mi dulcissime,*
With longing sighs I must entreat:	*Spes suspirantis animae,*
For you my loving tears are spent,	*Te quaerunt piae lacrymae,*
With heartfelt cries my soul is rent.	*Te clamor mentis intimae.*
Though I may wander far and wide,	*Quocunque loco fuero,*
I want my Jesus by my side.	*Meum Iesum desidero.*
What joy to find that he is near!	*Quam laetus, cum invenero!*
What comfort now to hold him here!	*Quam felix, cum tenuero!*
Then the embrace, and kisses, too,	*Tunc amplexus, tunc oscula,*
Better than cups of sweetest dew.	*Quae vincunt mellis pocula,*
Happy union with Christ at last!	*Tunc felix Christi copula;*
But all these things so quickly pass.	*Sed in his parva morula.*
Him whom I sought so long, I see,	*Iam quod quaesivi, video,*
Now I embrace him tenderly.	*Quod concupivi teneo;*
From love of Jesus I am spent;	*Amore Iesu langueo,*
My whole heart by fire is rent.	*Et corde totus ardeo.*
When he is held as such a prize,	*Iesus cum sic diligitur,*
This love for Jesus never dies:	*Hic amor non exstinguitur,*
It does not end but always grows;	*Non tepescit, nec moritur;*
Indeed it always burns and glows.	*Plus crescit et accenditur.*
This love's enkindled constantly	*Hic amor ardet jugiter,*
And sweetens all things wondrously:	*Dulcessit mirabiliter,*
It gives a taste for true delight,	*Sapit delectabiliter,*
Brings happiness to greater height.	*Delectat et feliciter.*
Heav'n-sent love has come to rest	*Hic amor missus coelitus,*
In deepest recess of my breast:	*Haeret mihi medullitus,*
With fire it sets my mind aflame,	*Mentem incendit penitus,*
My soul with joy too great to name.	*Hoc delectatur spiritus.*
O, what sweet and blessed fire,	*O beatum incendium,*
O, what ardent true desire!	*O ardens desiderium!*
O, dear consolation won	*O dulce refrigerium,*
To love him who is God's own Son!	*Amare Dei Filium!*

Flower of Virgin-Mother true,
And our beloved, dear Jesu:
Worship divine be yours alone
As you assume your royal throne!

Iesu, flos Matris Virginis,
Amor nostrae dulcedinis,
Tibi laus honor numinis,
Regnum beatitudinis.

O come, most noble King, we wait,
Father of glory vastly great.
Give to those who contemplate
All the splendor they await.

Veni, veni, Rex optime,
Pater immensae gloriae,
Affulge menti clarius
Iam exspectatus saepius.

Brighter, Jesus, than sunlight calm,
More pleasant than a fragrant balm,
Of all sweet things you are the best,
More lovable than all the rest.

Iesu, sole serenior,
Et balsamo suavior,
Omni dulcore dulcior,
Prae cunctis amabilior.

My every sense and taste is filled,
All yearning of my heart is stilled;
Nought else has power to entice,
Beloved only will suffice.

Cuius gustus sic afficit,
Cuius odor sic reficit.
In qua mens mea deficit:
Solus amanti sufficit.

You, the mind's true delectation,
You, love's longed-for consum-
mation;
My glory I discern in you,
Jesus, the world's salvation true.

Tu mentis delectatio,
Amoris consummatio;

Tu, mea gloriatio,
Iesu mundi salvatio.

Beloved, to your home return:
A place at Father's right you earn;
You have vanquished the ancient
foe—
So to your reign in heav'n now go.

Mi dilecte, revertere,
Consors paternae dexterae,
Hostem vicisti prospere,

Iam coeli regno fruere.

Where you ascend, I too must be.
You cannot e'er be far from me,
For you have carried off my heart.
In Jesus' praises all take part.

Sequar te quoquo ieris,
Mihi tolli non poteris;
Cum meum cor abstuleris,
Iesu laus nostri generis.

Celestial court, go forth to greet;
Throw wide your gates with praises
meet,
And to the conquering Hero sing,
"Jesus, all hail! The glorious King!

Coeli cives, occurrite,
Portas vestras attollite,

Triumphatori dicite:
Ave, Iesu Rex inclyte.

"King of all splendor, King of
   might,
Conquering King of triumph bright!
Giver of grace with lavish hand
And honor of the heavenly band!

"You, the one source of mercy's
   stream,
You, true light of heaven's gleam:
Drive clouds of sorrow out of sight
By giving us your glorious light!"

Celestial choirs all sing your praise,
Their echoed songs they ever raise.
Jesus brings joy down to our earth:
Our peace with God is brought to
   birth.

Jesus now reigns, peace to bestow—
A peace surpassing all I know.
Such peace is my heart's true desire;
I hasten, longing to acquire.

To his Father he makes his way
To exercise celestial sway.
And my heart, too, is gone from me,
That where he is, I too may be.

Let us now follow with our praise,
Songs, prayers, and hymns to Jesus
   raise,
That he may grant to us above
For ever to enjoy his love. Amen.

Rex virtutum, Rex gloriae,

Rex insignis victoriae,
Iesu largitor gratiae,
Honor coelestis curiae!

Tu, fons misericordiae,

Tu, verae lumen patriae;
Pelle nubem tristitiae,
Nobis dans lucem gloriae.

Te coeli chorus praedicat,
Et tuas laudes replicat;
Iesus orbem laetificat,
Et nos Deo pacificat.

Iesus in pace imperat,
Quae omnem sensum superat;
Hanc mens mea desiderat
Et illo frui properat.

Iesus ad Patrem rediit,
Coeleste regnum subiit,
Cor meum a me transit,
Post Jesum simul abiit.

Iam prosequamur laudibus,
Iesum, hymnis et precibus:

Ut nos donet coelestibus,
Cum ipso frui sedibus. Amen.